1.95

76-715

history

and

trends

literature for children

Pose Lamb
Consulting Editor
Purdue University

Storytelling and Creative Drama—*Dewey W. Chambers, University of the Pacific, Stockton, California*

Illustrations in Children's Books—*Patricia Cianciolo, Michigan State University*

Enrichment Ideas—*Ruth Kearney Carlson, California State College at Hayward*

History and Trends—*Margaret C. Gillespie, Marquette University*

Poetry in the Elementary School—*Virginia Witucke, Purdue University*

Its Discipline and Content—*Bernice Cullinan, New York University*

Children's Literature in the Curriculum—*Mary Montebello, State University of New York at Buffalo*

history
and
trends

MARGARET C. GILLESPIE
Marquette University

Pose Lamb
Consulting Editor
Purdue University

WM. C. BROWN COMPANY PUBLISHERS
Dubuque, Iowa

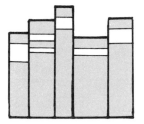

contents

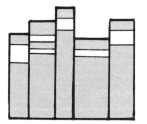

foreword

This series of books came to be because of the editor's conviction that most textbooks about literature for children had not been written for elementary teachers, regardless of the anticipated audience suggested by the titles. The words, *Literature for Children*, preceding each individual title indicate not only the respect for the field held by the authors and the editor but our evaluation of the importance of this type of literature, worthy of consideration along with other categories or classifications of English literature. However, it is *what happens* through books, and the *uses* of literature which are of concern to the authors of this series, as well as the provision of an historical perspective and some knowledge of the writer's and the illustrator's crafts. Our work, then, is directed primarily to the elementary classroom teacher who wants to design and implement an effective program of literature for children.

Because entire books have been devoted to specific topics, for example, the history of literature for children, it is hoped that such topics are covered in greater depth than usual. They are not merely books *about* children's literature; the focus in this series is on helping teachers see what literature for children has been, the direction or directions pointed by scholars in the field, and some ways in which a teacher can share with children the excitement and joy of reading. The authors have tried to share with teachers and prospective teachers their enthusiasm for children's literature, today's and yesterday's; for an unenthusiastic teacher, though well-informed, will not communicate enthusiasm to his pupils.

The author of each book was selected, first because he has demonstrated this enthusiasm in his teaching and writing, and secondly because of his competence in the field of children's literature in general. It is hoped that the thoroughness and depth with which each topic has been explored and the expertise which each author has brought to a topic in which he has a particular interest will serve as sufficient justifications for such a venture.

Children's literature courses are among the most popular courses in the professional sequence at many colleges and universities. It is rewarding and exciting to re-enter the world of literature for children, to experience again the joy of encountering a new author or of renewing acquaintance with a favorite author or a character created by an author.

The editor and the authors of this series have tried to capture the magic that is literature for children and to provide some help for teachers who want to share that *magic with children*.

To note that one can better understand where he *is* if he knows where he's *been* is in the nature of repeating a truism, if not a cliché. Nevertheless, some understanding of the history of children's literature should lead to deeper appreciation of the quality and quantity of the literature made available to children today. Twentieth century children have a wealth of *good literary material* from which to select. In this respect, as in others, they are far more fortunate than the children of earlier generations.

Writers for children are inevitably influenced by the times in which they live. The views held about children—are they evil, needing to have devils exorcised? animals, subject to clearly defined laws of reinforcement and training? inherently good, until spoiled by society?—these views determine the purpose for which authors write. Other influences are, of course, the prevailing social and economic conditions of a period. One of the reasons for selecting the title of this series, *Literature for Children,* relates to the belief that this facet of literature is no less respectable and no less deserving of serious study than any other. Dr. Gillespie makes it very clear that all of the trends and all of the influences which impinge upon an author who directs his material toward an adult audience also affect the writer for children. She presents a thought-provoking anaylsis of *why* books for children were as they were and are as they are. This book is more than a survey of what books for children were written and published when, and by whom, although this information is not neglected.

Specifically, the reader will find the author's discussion of the following questions or issues stimulating and the reference lists helpful in finding additional data and/or points of view:

What initiated publishers' interest in producing books for children? How were the earliest books for children marketed? Who sold them and where were they sold?

Are there types of books which have been popular with children for a considerable period of time, or do children's tastes in literature change with some regularity and rapidity? Are there *classics* in children's literature? If so, which books are most deserving of this accolade?

What major changes have occurred in children's books since the seventeenth century? Have these changes been substantive or primarily improvements in illustrations, format, and printing techniques?

In Margaret Gillespie's words, *There were tales to tell,* and her discussion of the course of literature for children is both interesting and enlightening.

Pose Lamb, Editor

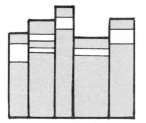

preface

It was with great temerity and naivete that this task was undertaken. It was with courage and increasing wisdom that the task was continued, and it was with awe, delight, pleasure, and gratitude that it was finally accomplished.

The awe was engendered by the vastness in terms of time, space, and quantity of books which forms the framework of the historical development of a literature for children. Added to this was the awesome and invaluable collection of historical writing and research in the field, a collection which had to be tapped.

The delight and pleasure, of course, was in discovering and rediscovering some of the tales, stories, poems, and illustrations which are found in the early collections and compilations. For example, Leonard de Vries truly culled *Flowers of Delight* from the Osborne Collection of Early Children's Books; John Ashton's compilation of chapbooks is an exciting adventure which takes the reader back in time; and the facsimile of John Newbery's *A Little Pretty Pocket-Book* brings the famous shop, *The Bible and Crown* near Devereux Court, into sharper focus as the reader shares the "Instruction and Amusement of Master Tommy and pretty Miss Polly."

The gratitude is most humbly offered to Barbara Kommer, Carolyn Bilous, Jeanne DesJardins, Gladys Eisele, Eva Lee Hinton, Jane Layman, Jeanne Nimori, and Debbie Zeeryp who searched, typed, checked, and rechecked indefatigably, rendering efficient, consistent, and cheerful aid.

A very special "mahalo" goes to those friendly librarians in the youth rooms of the Hawaii State Library and the Milwaukee Public Library, especially to Margaret Smith at the University of Hawaii Library, for their interest, kindness, and help; and to Ancy McFadden, my production editor, who kept me both motivated and accurate.

M. C. G.

Photograph courtesy of Margaret Glaser.

chapter 1

introduction—
it took a long time

Upon entering the youth room in the central library of a large metropolitan city in the Middle West, one is instantly struck by the spaciousness and the beckoning atmosphere which is subtly conveyed. It is indeed a place to become *Hooked on Books,* a place of warmth and welcome where the young person can discover and enjoy the satisfactions and delights to be obtained from reading good books.

No drab and forbidding stacks meet the eye here. One is immediately drawn to the spacious and gracious arrangements for browsing and reading groupings. The Three Bears come to mind as one notices the "large chairs, the small chairs, and the middle size chairs" placed around tables of proportionate height. There are round tables, rectangular tables, couches, and benches. There are window benches with cushioned seats and wrought-iron backs which serve as trays on which to rest and display books. Sofas and lounging chairs are grouped around lovely planters or tables on which may be placed statuary such as the replica of a reclining Gulliver with the little Lilliputians resting on his arms.

Color abounds in the upholstery. Greens, whites, and persimmons are artfully blended to please the eye rather than to offend it. Bulletin board displays—colorful and meaningful—draw the visitor so that he may find out where to GO PLACES WITH BOOKS. There is an almost life-size cutout of the lion from James Daugherty's *Andy and the Lion.* On his back is a boy engrossed in reading J. Allen Bosworth's *All the Dark Places.* A young girl sprawls on the floor at the lion's forepaws reading about *Ramona the Pest,* one of Beverly Cleary's well-loved series' characters. It would be nice to have every child a part of this group. Another eye-catcher, on an adjoining board, admonishes the reader to SOLVE YOUR PUZZLES—READ. Book jackets on this board arouse curiosity about Gallant's, *Exploring the Moon,* Hutchins' *This Is a Flower,* and *The Wonderful World of Energy* by Lancelot Hogben.

1

And then the books—books to the right of us, books to the left of us and fore and aft of us volley and thunder their appeals as impressively as did Tennyson's cannons. All shapes and sizes of covers, pictures, print, and content. For the beginning reader, many picture books are displayed along the trays and on the tables. One glimpses among the many eye-catchers Freeman's *Mop Top,* the Emberleys' Caldecott winner, *Drummer Hoff,* and that perennial favorite, *Billy and Blaze,* by C. W. Anderson. The shelves, not too high for these young readers, are well marked and the spaces between are wide enough to permit plenty of room for light and air and for the young people to wander through. It is easy to learn the arrangement. The picture story books are shelved near the "wee" tables. Holiday books are grouped nearby. Children's fiction, alphabetically shelved according to authors, fills the next aisles. This is followed by a section for biography, folktales, legends, and informational books on history, science, and so forth.

The books that are "too good to miss" according to Arbuthnot and others, all of the rungs on the Reading Ladders published by the American Council on Education, collections of poems, folktales—all are here for the asking. There are books of fiction both fanciful and realistic, and biographies of great men and women who have lived before our time, such as Cornelia Meigs' *Invincible Louisa* which tells about the author of that all time favorite of girls, *Little Women,* and Catherine Owens Pearce's fine recounting of the accomplishments of Helen Keller. One can make the acquaintance of Benjamin Franklin, Abraham Lincoln, John F. Kennedy, and other memorable figures in our country's history. There are stories which have special appeal to the varying tastes of individuals: mystery stories, sports stories, stories about animals, science fiction, and stories of sheer nonsense just for fun and laughter. Collections of poems, folk and fairy tales, and legends may be browsed through to find old favorites or to cultivate new ones. Youngsters whose minds are thirsty for knowledge will find a wealth of books which inform, expand, and explain literally everything under the sun.

Caldecott, Newbery, and other award winning books have a special place, as well they should. Let's look at the Caldecott award winner, *Drummer Hoff,* adapted by Barbara Emberley and illustrated by Ed Emberley. Bright primary colors are used to portray the cannon, Drummer Hoff (who will fire it off!), and his superiors who will aid and abet him in the act. The old-world flavor of the simple, repetitious tale, as well as its humor, are superbly blended in text and picture. "When General Border gave the order," the ensuing "Kahbahbloomph" resounds across two full pages in a riot of colorful mayhem that exceeds anticipation.

Here is a Newbery award winner, *From the Mixed-Up Files of Mrs. Basil E. Frankweiler* by E. L. Konigsberg. This intriguing adventure of two children of modern suburban culture contains excitement, drama, and unusual turns of events which satisfy their adventurous peers in real life. Claudia, the shrewd one, has the urge to run away but invites her thrifty younger brother to share the escapade, for both social and economic reasons. She eschews the painful hardships of the typical "take-to-the-road" runaway; instead she chooses the relative warmth and comfort of the Metropolitan Museum which offers a lovely "museum piece" bed in which to rest. Of course, if you are "on the lam," you must get up early and hide in the rest room, where you stand on the toilet seat so that your feet are not visible while these rooms are being checked by the guards. Running away proves to be an experience which keeps Claudia on her mettle, and it is how the two children come to see and be fascinated with the "Angel," the statue which is drawing many people to the museum. It is their curiosity about "Angel," which leads them to Mrs. Frankweiler, who holds the secret to the "Angel" in her "mixed-up files."

And so this book haven, a place of anticipation and promise, offers a feast—a smorgasbord—to satisfy the wide variety of tastes of the young patrons for whom it is intended. Whatever the limits, two books a week, maybe four, it rarely satisfies the gourmet readers and those whose appetites are growing. Wrenching decisions must be made as to which books to choose and which to leave for another day.

Librarians

The librarians, the friendly and understanding people who help the children with their decisions and their indecisions, are key figures in this book world. The plot of many stories revolves around this relationship between librarians and children. For example, there is Sue Felt's story of *Rosa-Too-Little* who so much wanted to draw books from the library when she was too little to do so. But she was welcomed and encouraged, and finally the time came when she could write her name and receive a library card of her very own. And a librarian gave sympathetic understanding to the stalwart and persistent young man who weathered a blizzard and became lost trying to find "Mike's House" in Julia Sauer's book of that name.

Sydney Taylor's *All-of-a-Kind Family* also were steady and responsible borrowers of books. When Sarah couldn't find her book on the day it was due, the librarian helped her solve the problem in a manner that was compatible with her financial ability. The solution was a relief to Sarah, and her admiration for the librarian was reinforced.

> Sarah clasped her hands together joyfully, "Oh thank you! I think you're the kindest library lady in the whole world." Miss Allen's smile was warm and friendly. . . .

"Sarah has never forgotten your kindness to her. For that matter,
all the children are always telling me such nice things about you.
How you're always ready with a suggestion about what they should
read and how interested you are in discussing the books with them.
I appreciate that." "It's a pleasure to help such eager readers," the
librarian said, smiling at the upturned faces.[1]

Librarians are faced with crucial problems just as the borrowers
are. In their relationships with their young patrons, there are often
sensitive decisions to make; and there are important decisions to make
in selecting titles for their collections as well. From the deluge of trade
books being published each year, they must make choices for their
young readers. Although reviews and many book selection aids are
available to them, they know that it will be the readers themselves who
will eventually affirm or negate these choices. The withdrawals are
the "proof of the pudding."

Book publishing for juveniles is a large enterprise in the United
States today. It accounts for 16 percent of all book sales. Only half as
many books for children were published twenty years ago, and that
was twice as many as were in circulation two decades before that.
This means that from approximately seven hundred books for children
being published in 1930, this number has grown to three thousand or
more being published now.[2]

It isn't surprising then that library circulation has increased with
this growing wealth of available books. Surveys of thirty-three libraries
in 1960 presented statistics to corroborate this fact.[3] These statistics
suggest that books for children as big business is a phenomenon of the
twentieth century. It all began with the oral traditions in the dim and
distant past, and it took a long time to grow.

Early Publishers

William Caxton was one of the earliest entrepreneurs in the publishing business. In 1476, at the sign of the Red Pole in Westminster,
near the Abbey, he published books at what, for that time, was a furious
pace when compared to the slow and painstaking rate at which manuscripts had been produced. He did not ignore the young readers. Manners and morals concerning behavior in the households of the great
were served in couplet and in rhyme to the young male reader in the
Book of Curtesye or Lytell John, which was brought out in 1477. *The
Knights of the Tower* followed in 1484. This one was for the girls—a
gentleman's instructions to his daughter. It is obvious from the titles
that Caxton, though he made one of the early efforts to address read-

[1]Sydney Taylor, *All-of-a-Kind Family,* illustrated by Helen John (Chicago:
Follett Publishing Co., 1951), p. 23, p. 66.
[2]Phyllis Steckler, ed., *Bowker Annual* (New York: R. R. Bowker Co., 1966).
[3]"Reading on the Rise," in *Time,* vol. 76, (July 25, 1960), p. 44.

ing material directly to children, was a man of his culture who believed
that books for children should instruct and improve them.

For the adults, Caxton published European romances, the works
of Chaucer, Langland, and Malory. It was Malory's *Morte d'Arthur*
which the children took unto themselves, of course, as they had taken
Aesop's Fables published one year before.

In the middle of the seventeenth century, chapmen (peddlers)
were carrying chapbooks on their peregrinations throughout the English countryside. These were inexpensive books, usually merely folded
and not stitched. Ribbons and laces were frequently inserted by the
owners. The books approximated 32-64 pages which contained thrills
and adventures galore.

One was about that worthy protagonist, Sir Bevis of Southampton,
who is cheated out of his birthright and sold to the Saracens; how he
encounters Ascapart, the thirty-foot giant, whose eyes are a foot apart.
Ascapart is vanquished by Bevis who spares his life on condition that
he become Bevis' servant. In ensuing adventures, Ascapart picks Bevis
up and carries him about like a toy, much to the great joy of young
readers.

Valentine's and Orson's adventures make up another "famous history" peddled by chapmen. These two brothers are separated in childhood. Valentine is brought up by the court, but Orson is carried off
by a bear. When the bear's four cubs do not devour Orson, the old
bear takes a fancy to him, and Orson grows up as a wild creature. Of
course, the two brothers encounter each other in the woods after they
have reached manhood. Unaware of their relationship, they engage in
physical combat. Valentine emerges victorious, proving that skill is more
important than strength. He subsequently tames Orson and teaches him
the arts of chivalry.

It has been related that James Boswell, at the age of twenty-one,
came upon some chapbooks in the London Printing Office in Bow
Churchyard. He purchased from among them some of his childhood
favorites and had then bound under the title, *Curious Productions*. In
contrast, John Bunyan, the devout Puritan and author of *Pilgrim's
Progress*, was reported to have confessed with some remorse that he
had in his youth been guilty of reading "George on Horseback," "Sir
Bevis of Southampton," and other fables found in John Ashton's *Chap-
Books of the Eighteenth Century*.

Richard Steele, who wrote under the pseudonym of Isaac Bickerstaffe
in the time of Queen Anne, wrote about his godson's interest in chapbooks in the No. 95 edition of the *Tatler*:

> I perceived him a very great historian in Aesop's Fables; but
> he frankly declared to me his mind, "that he did not delight in that
> learning, because he did not believe that they were true;" for which
> reason I found that he had very much turned his studies for about

a twelve-month past, into the lives and adventures of Don Bellianis of Greece, Guy of Warwick, the Seven Champions, and other historians of that age. . . .[4]

Though chapbooks could not boast of literary style since they were for the most part linguistically and aesthetically poor in quality, they had plots which afforded thrills and adventures to harmonize with the adventurous natures of the purchasers.

It would appear that Richard Steele's tolerance for his godson's taste in reading was very atypical for this period when society sanctioned only those books for children which served as a vehicle for imparting religious, moral, and scholastic lessons. Some of these books contained lurid examples of the snares of Satan and taught that death and damnation would be the consequence of "ungodly" behavior. The following annotations illustrate their dismal and dreary content:

> Crossman, Samuel. The young mans monitor. Or a modest offer toward the pious, and virtuous composure of life from youth to riper years. (1664) . . . Crossman says, "to settle the great case of your Souls heavenword" through regeneration. "*You came hither* to seek the Lord, and his face" (p. 22). The truly virtuous young man never reviles religion or religious people; he never gambles, breaks the Sabbath, speaks vainly, lies, swears, takes the name of the Lord in vain, or abuses himself with drink. The truly virtuous young man rather chooses "the fear of the Lord with his whole heart," delights in the Bible, follows diligently some honest calling, is "easily contented with almost any food and raiment," is modest and chaste, wisely lays up "all the memorable experiences and observations of his Youth for the better instruction of his riper years," and grows daily in virtue as in stature (ch. 6-7). "Awake then I beseech you, for the Lords sake; while it is yet the morning of your life, the flower of your years" (p. 244).[5]

> Janeway, James. A token for children, being an exact account of the conversion, holy and exemplary lives and joyful deaths of several young children. By James Janeway, minister of the gospel. To which is added, a token for the children of New-England, or, some examples of children, in whom the fear of God was remarkably budding before they died; in several parts of New England. Preserved and published for the encouragement of piety in other children. (1671)[6]

> Peck, Samuel. A new-years gift for youth: being the substance of a sermon preached at the funeral of Mrs. Elizabeth Bell (aged sixteen years, odd months), at St. Mary, Overies, Decemb. 1, 1686, upon these words (chosen by her) of Solomon's, Eccles. 12. 1., Remember thy Creator in the days of thy youth, etc. 1687.[7]

---

[4]Percy Muir, *English Children's Books: 1600-1900.* (New York: Frederick A. Praeger, Publishers, 1954), p. 23.

[5]William Sloane, *Children's Books in England and America in the Seventeenth Century* (New York: King's Crown Press, Columbia University Press, 1955), pp. 162-3.

[6]Ibid., pp. 166-7.

[7]Ibid., p. 200.

In a similar vein, some of the earliest coverless works available for American children in the seventeenth century were *Remember Thy Creator in the Days of Thy Youth,* and *Spiritual Milk for Boston Babes.* Other books to follow were *War with the Devil; or the Young Man's Conflict with the Powers of Darkness* and *The New-England Primer.* Compare the following excerpts from two children's books.

> In Adam's Fall
> We sinned all.
>
> Thy Life to Mend
> This Book Attend.
>
> The Cat doth play
> And after slay.
>
> The Idle Fool
> Is whipt at School.
>
> Time cuts down all
> Both great and small.
>
> Xerxes the great did die,
> And so must you & I.[8]

The above rhymes are from the alphabet pages of *The New-England Primer* first published in 1690. Thirty thousand copies were sold during its century of use. It is typical of the grim, didactic, and moralistc reading fare for children in that period.

In contrast try:

> The Duchess sang happily, "I'm going to make
> A lovely light luscious delectable cake."
> She stirred the ingredients, all in a flutter,
> In went the sugar and flour and butter,
> In went the almonds, the raisins, the suet;
> She added some vinegar and dropped in the cruet.
> She added the yeast, six times for good measure.
> (A light fluffy cake is really a pleasure.)
> She added some eggs, several dozen, well-beaten,
> And some left-over pudding that they hadn't eaten.
> Blueberries, gooseberries, cranberries, hogberries,
> Blackberries, mulberries, burberries, dogberries;
> Peppermint, cinnamon, laurel and squill,
> Wintergreen, nutmeg, angelica, dill—
> Whatever she found she put into the batter,
> And what she left out didn't really much matter.
> Then she added more yeast—it seemed like a ton—
> She stirred it together and the mixture was done.[9]

---

[8]Paul Leicester Ford, ed., *The New-England Primer* (New York: Teachers College Press, Teachers College, Columbia University, 1962).

[9]Virginia Kahl, *The Duchess Bakes a Cake* (New York: Charles Scribner's Sons, 1955).

Here is Virginia Kahl's delightful Duchess who baked that "lovely light luscious delectable cake." Fanciful ideas, exciting color, and laughter are imbedded in this gay tale as opposed to the somber, self-abasement of the alphabet rhymes in the primer. How did those little children of the seventeenth century ever learn the alphabet or come to appreciate that reading is a satisfying experience?

John Newbery came upon the scene in 1744. He was probably not the first publisher of books exclusively for children, since evidence shows that a few books preceded him and also that a few were being published concomitantly. Thomas Boreman, for example, published *The Gigantick Histories* in 1740. These books were extremely small, about two inches in length, and were gaily decorated with covers of Dutch flowered paper.

At about the same time, a Mrs. Mary Cooper published *The Child's New Plaything.* Though this was an alphabet and spelling book, there were traditional rhymes, such as "A Apple Pie," and there were short adaptations of *St. George, Guy of Warwick,* and other Medieval folktales.[10]

Newbery has achieved everlasting fame, however, as being the first publisher openly to avow "amusement" as an important response to be sought by children through their reading. On June 18th of 1744, an advertisement was published in the "Penny London Morning Advertiser."

> This Day is publish'd According to Act of Parliament (Neatly bound and gilt)
> A LITTLE PRETTY POCKET-BOOK, intended for the Instruction and Amusement of little Master Tommy and pretty Miss Polly; with an agreeable Letter to each from *Jack the Giant-Killer;* as also a Ball and Pincushion, the Use of which will infallibly make Tommy a good Boy and Polly a good Girl.
> To the Whole is prefix'd, A Lecture on Education, humbly address'd to all Parents, Guardians, Governesses, etc.; wherein Rules are laid down for making their children strong, hardy, healthy, virtuous, wise, and happy. . . .
> Printed for J. Newbery, at the *Bible and Crown,* near Devereux Court, without Temple Bar. Price of the Book alone 6d., with Ball or Pincushion 8d.[11]

In the century of enlightenment in which Newbery lived, ability to read the Bible was still considered the major purpose for learning to read. John Locke's theories were making an impact on educators and writers. It appears that John Newbery was impressed with Locke's ideas about learning through play and with his statements that children

---

[10]John Newbery, *A Little Pretty Pocket-Book* (New York: Harcourt, Brace & World, 1967), p. 13.
[11]Ibid., p. 2.

should learn to read through "pleasant" books. *A Little Pretty Pocket-Book* incorporated Locke's ideas of games and pleasure, but it also contained manners, morals, and lessons, albeit phrased in rhyme, jingles, and games.

Newbery attracted the young readers of the time with bright flowered and gilt paper covers. He founded a very prosperous business with his medleys of morals and lessons. The Newbery books were all issued anonymously or under pseudonyms. The famous *History of Little Goody Two Shoes,* published in 1765, became a minor classic among his publications. Twenty-two books for the "Instruction and Amusement of Children" are listed in the facsimile of *A Little Pretty Pocket-Book,* one of the volumes in the *Milestones in Children's Literature* series. Though this is not a complete summary of his publications, it bears testimony to Newbery's right to the honor of having his name given to the award for the most distinguished children's book of the year, The John Newbery Medal Award.

Though children had the lovely folk and fairy tales, by fair or surreptitious means, throughout much of modern historical times, and though they chose what they liked from adult literature, their choices were very limited. The content of a library for children, if indeed they had a library—and public ones did not exist—were pitifully barren as compared with our present-day collections, despite the efforts of Newbery and his fellow publishers. The question, from early colonial times down to the beginning of the twentieth century, might have been "What books are there for children?" rather than "What do I choose to read from these thousands of books?", a question that might be asked today.

And that is the way it was. A few attempts at breakthroughs were made, but patterns of didacticism and moralistic preaching at children were so thoroughly ingrained in the culture that it was not until the middle of the nineteenth century that joy and laughter were brought into children's books. Then Lewis Carroll held up the looking-glass and let children roam in a land of make-believe where manners and modes were prescribed according to the wishes of the inhabitants.

This book, then, will present a brief historical background of children's literature, emphasizing the books that children *read,* whether the authors' intentions were to write for children, or whether their books were addressed to adults. This world of children's literature *has been* and *continues to be* one that is dominated by children's choices. In ancient times, children and adults alike shared in the tales embodying ideas which men developed as they attempted to explain the natural and spiritual forces which impinged upon them. Those tales which have survived through the ages demonstrate the imagination and poetic qualities inherent in the folklore.

Some teaching and lesson books of earlier centuries are pertinent to the discussion since they constituted the major reading fare of the time. There will be no attempt, however, to treat the historical development of teaching books per se. The discussion here will focus, rather, on the history and content of children's literature as an artistic discipline.

QUESTIONS AND SUGGESTIONS

1. Visit the youth room in a public library in your community. Describe the physical setting. Notice the bulletin boards, posters, displays, and other "invitations to reading." Compare the youth room to the adult reading and reference room.

2. Visit a school library. Observe the physical and psychological climate. What do you observe in the environment which suggests that a wide span of children's ages and reading interests are being accommodated?

3. Try to arrange a visit with a children's librarian. Discuss with her the job responsibilities in relation to book selection and service to children's interests and reading growth.

4. How might knowledge of the historical background of children's literature aid the librarian, the teacher, and the student in their understanding and appreciation of children's books?

SELECTED REFERENCES FOR CHILDREN

ALCOTT, LOUISA MAY. *Little Women*. New York: Thomas Y. Crowell, 1955, 1868.

ANDERSON, C. W. *Billy and Blaze*. New York: Macmillan Co., 1962.

BOSWORTH, J. ALLEN. *All the Dark Places*. Garden City, N.Y.: Doubleday & Co., 1968.

CLEARY, BEVERLY. *Ramona the Pest*. New York: William Morrow & Co., 1968.

DAUGHERTY, JAMES. *Andy and the Lion*. New York: Viking Press, 1938.

EMBERLEY, BARBARA. *Drummer Hoff*. Illustrated by Ed Emberley. Englewood Cliffs, N. J.: Prentice-Hall, 1967.

FELT, SUE. *Rosa-Too-Little*. Garden City, N.Y.: Doubleday & Co., 1950.

FORD, PAUL LEICESTER, ed. *The New-England Primer*. New York: Teachers College Press, Teachers College, Columbia University, 1962.

FREEMAN, DON. *Mop Top*. New York: Viking Press, 1955.

GALLANT, ROY A. *Exploring the Moon*. Garden City, N.Y.: Doubleday & Co., 1966.

HOGBEN, LANCELOT. *The Wonderful World of Energy*. Garden City, N.Y.: Doubleday & Co., 1968.

HUTCHINS, ROSS. *This Is a Flower*. New York: Dodd, Mead & Co., 1963.

KAHL, VIRGINIA. *The Duchess Bakes a Cake*. New York: Charles Scribner's Sons, 1955.

KONIGSBERG, E. L. *From the Mixed-Up Files of Mrs. Basil E. Frankweiler*. New York: Atheneum Publishers, 1967.

MEIGS, CORNELIA. *Invincible Louisa*. Boston: Little, Brown & Co., 1961, 1963.
PEARCE, CATHERINE OWENS. *The Helen Keller Story*. New York: Thomas Y. Crowell, 1959.
SAUER, JULIA. *Mike's House*. Illustrated by Don Freeman. New York: Viking Press, 1954.
TAYLOR, SYDNEY. *All-of-a-Kind Family*. Illustrated by Helen John. Chicago: Follett Publishing Co., 1951.

SELECTED CHAPTER REFERENCES

AESOP. *Five Centuries of Illustrated Fables*. Selected by John McKendry. Greenwich, Conn.: New York Graphic Society, 1964.
ASHTON, JOHN, *Chap-Books of the Eighteenth Century*. New York: Benjamin Blom, 1966.
BOREMAN, THOMAS. *The Gigantick Histories*. London: Thomas Boreman, 1740.
BUNYAN, JOHN. *Pilgrim's Progress*. 1st ed. London: 1676.
CAXTON, WILLIAM. *Book of Courtesye or Lytyll John*. London: Caxton, 1477.
———. *The Knights of the Tower*. London: Caxton, 1484.
COOPER, MRS. MARY. *The Child's New Plaything*. London: Cooper, 1743.
FADER, DANIEL N., and McNEILL, ELTON B. *Hooked on Books*. New York: G. P. Putnam's Sons, 1968.
KEACH, BENJAMIN. *War with the Devil; or the Young Man's Conflict with the Powers of Darkness*. New York: 1707.
MALORY, SIR THOMAS. *Morte d'Arthur*. London: Caxton, 1485.
MUIR, PERCY. *English Children's Books: 1600-1900*. New York: Frederick A. Praeger, Publishers, 1954.
NEWBERY, JOHN. *A Little Pretty Pocket-Book*. New York: Harcourt, Brace & World, 1967.
No Author. *The History of Little Goody Two Shoes*. London: Newbery, 1766.
"Reading on the Rise," in *Time*, vol. 76, (July 25, 1960), p. 44.
SLOANE, WILLIAM. *Children's Books in England and America in the Seventeenth Century*. New York: King's Crown Press, Columbia University Press, 1955.
STECKLER, PHYLLIS, ed., *Bowker Annual*. New York: R. R. Bowker Co., 1966.

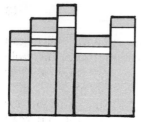

chapter 2

great men, great thoughts —
little books, little lessons

Most historians of children's literature agree that books written specifically for the child are a modern development in the field of writing and publishing. Some have even suggested that the child as a person, with his own unique behaviors and needs, is a modern development, too.[1]

Though both of these statements may be oversimplification and generalization of fact, a study of the historical development of children's literature reflects the paucity of interest and effort in the field of writing directed to the child consumer until the middle of the nineteenth century. William Caxton, Thomas Boreman, and John Newbery were among the notable exceptions in their attempts to "please the little masters and mistresses." The most significant appeals to children in their books, however, were in format, illustrations, and style of writing. They seem to have been sensitive to the fact that the young child sought amusement and entertainment in literary fare, but they were shackled by the prevailing attitudes toward children and the societal values of the times. Their books were small in size, because they thought this was in keeping with the size of the child; and their books contained gay little illustrations to captivate the young reader's interest. However, though the books were watered down and were couched in catchy rhymes, moralizing and didacticism were imbedded in them.

It remains a moot question as to whether or not Caxton, Boreman, and Newbery would have published books solely for children's entertainment had there been no threat to their commercial interests. It does seem certain that their keen business acumen made them sensitive to the tenor of the times. After all, the parents did control the sixpences of the young purchasers. This circumstance mitigated against the sale of books sans morals and lessons.

[1]Bess Porter Adams, *About Books and Children* (New York: Holt, Rinehart & Winston, 1953), p. 4.

Lewis Carroll's tale, published in 1864, of the immortal Alice and her adventures after following the white rabbit down into his hole seems to be the real landmark in modern literature for children. This is the first instance of a book's being written for no other purpose than for the sheer pleasure it gave the author as he wove the yarn and for the pleasure that it gave to his audience as they listened to it and read it. It would appear that finally, after many long and dreary centuries of having been fed manners, morals, lessons, and adult fare as a literary diet, children were beginning to come into their own.

But let us peer back into time—into the time when the Bible was the only book which the child possessed; and let us look back even farther, to the time before the invention of printing, to the time when the art of reading was preserved by a mere handful of monks who kept thought and existing knowledge alive through their teaching and writing of manuscripts. Obviously, there were no books written at that time for the sheer enjoyment of the child. The very precious few, written with such labor and toil, were for instructional purposes—to preserve and disseminate knowledge. Children handled these books infrequently. More often, the monk-tutor held the delicate parchment sheets or rolls for the students to see as he taught the lessons which they contained.

An Outer Monastic School. Reproduced from Ellwood P. Cubberley's *History of Education*, by permission of Houghton Mifflin Company.

The historical development of a literature for children is closely interwoven and related to the changing patterns of educational thought. Political, economic, and religious factors are fundamental influences in establishing the cultural patterns and values of a society. Educational thought is molded through the interaction of these societal forces. Prevailing attitudes toward children are revealed in the religious and educational philosophies and in the patterns of transmitting the cultural values of any given period.

Early European Beginnings

After the decline of the Roman Empire, man was engaged in attempting "to organize a new society, to acquire the rudiments of culture and to give expression to his feelings in artistic creation."[2] As has been suggested, education and culture were kept alive primarily through the efforts of the monastics of the time. There were few books except textbooks and books containing compilations of existing knowledge in a variety of disciplines. These were painstakingly handwritten by monks, in the dark, damp cells of the monasteries spread throughout Europe. Hundreds of hours were spent on producing each work. The problem of obtaining the expensive parchment on which they were written was another limiting factor. Thus, the scarcity of books for common consumption is understandable. This dearth of books is highlighted in the writing of Mrs. Field as she tells about the library of the Canterbury School established in the year 668.

> Theodore of Tarsus—founded his great and long famous school and endowed it with a "noble library" of some half dozen volumes, including "a splendid Homer" on paper, a rare and most valuable possesion.[3]

During this period, and in succeeding centuries, children were looked upon as little adults. They were dressed according to the image and likeness of their adult counterparts. Moreover, their activities and behavior were also expected to conform to these adult models. What was good for adults was also considered good for children. It follows that this rationale was also true of literary pursuits. From these early times until the middle of the nineteenth century, most books for children were written for the purpose of instruction in matters of temporal knowledge and religious precepts which, it was believed, would prepare the child for adulthood.

A review of the educational thought as revealed in the writings of the leading scholars and philosophers of these centuries reveals much information about the historical development of a literature for children.

Aldhelm. An English monk, Aldhelm, who lived from 640-709, is credited with having written the first lesson book for children, *De Septenario, de Metris, Enigmatibus, ad Pedum Regulus.* Even a minimal acquaintance with Latin suggests that this book had lessons and puzzles about the number seven, perhaps some riddles, and surely some verses, "Metris." The style of the book was that of question and answer dialogue, a form popular with the monks of that time.

---

[2]Robert Ulich, *History of Educational Thought* (New York: Litton Educational Publishing, by permission of Van Nostrand Reinhold Co., 1950, 1945), p. 89.
[3]Mrs. Elizabeth M. Field, *The Child and His Book* (London: Wells Gardner, 1891), p. 16.

Venerable Bede. Aldhelm was followed by another famous scribe, the Venerable Bede (673-735), a most prolific writer of forty-five books in his lifetime. This seems like a formidable task when one considers that these manuscripts were produced during long hours of fatiguing labor. Much of the content was a recapitulation and reminiscence of the scholarly treatises of Plato, Aristotle, St. Augustine, and others, rather than his own original work. This dedication to the preservation of accumulated knowledge throughout these illiterate years was a rewarding contribution to mankind. One of his most famous manuscripts was entitled *De Natura Rerum.* It contained information on natural science, history, astronomy, and botany. This manuscript served as a textbook for English youth for more than three hundred years.

Bede often used allegories in his writing to present facts about grammar, rhetoric, music, and mathematics. The following mathematical problem, believed to have been written by Bede and taken from a tenth or eleventh century manuscript, demonstrates his attempt to interest the student.

> An old man met a child. "Good day, my son," says he; "may you live as long as you have lived, and as much more, and thrice as much as all this, and if God give you one year in addition to the others, you will be just a century old." What was the lad's age?[4]

Alcuin. Egbert, first king of the English people, founded a famous school at York. Here he furthered the cause of education in those dim and long ago days (? — 766) by collecting works of Bede, Aldhelm, and Orosius, an authority on history, as well as copies of the writings of Greek and Roman authors. It was to this monastery at York that Alcuin came (735-804). Alcuin is remembered as being the tutor of Charlemagne's sons at the court of Aachen. He wrote a variety of school textbooks in which he used colorful figures of speech. For example, he called grass "the garment of the earth," and a traveler was "one who leaves no footsteps."[5]

Ælfric. One of the last great Anglo-Saxon teachers before William the Conqueror invaded England in 1066 was Ælfric (955-1020?). He was renowned as the "Grammarian" because of his Latin-English dictionary, the *Vocabulary.* This dictionary was used for the next four hundred years. In those days, and continuing into modern times, Latin was considered to be the language of erudition, and young boys were forced to speak Latin in the monastery schools even during play hours.

The *Colloquy,* another famous schoolbook written by Ælfric, had a question and answer format as the title suggests. This, according to him, made the lessons about daily living "simple and pleasant" for the students.

---

[4]Venerable Bede, cited in Adams, *About Books and Children,* p. 10.
[5]Adams, *About Books and Children,* p. 11.

The Renaissance

Among the results of the Crusades of the eleventh and twelfth centuries in Europe were the breakdown of the great empires, the rise of towns and of middle class society, and the return of Aristotle to Western culture.

Throughout historical times in western Europe and America, education has been dependent upon industry, commerce, and urban prosperity. The Crusades were responsible for stimulating and renewing trade with the East. Through these renewed contacts, the works of Plato, Aristotle, and other writers were re-introduced into Europe.

This recovery of classical learning, and a movement throughout Europe called the humanistic movement, which sought self-realization and self-expression, gave great impetus to the development of schools and the quest for knowledge. This humanistic movement stressed the importance of the individual in the secular world as opposed to the former religious orientation and preoccupation with preparation for life after death. It led to the rise of the middle class with its guilds and towns. People were eager for knowledge, and Cathedral universities were spreading throughout Europe. Common schools arose in the towns. Lesson books for children began to be written in the vernacular.

Books of this period, therefore, stressed human achievement—the works of man. There developed a literature of knowledge and also a literature of power. Dramatic, epic, oratorical, and philosophical works of writers who were concerned with form as well as with the teaching aspects of the content became part of the curriculum of the culture. The sonnet as a literary art form came into being. Human life and values were stressed. The literature of the Italian Renaissance expressed interest in aesthetic experience and conduct, and in the political life of the period. Dante's *Divine Comedy,* as well as the verse of Petrarch and Boccacio, were written during this time.

The more liberal education emphasized human freedom and individual freedom. Piety, instead of being the major cultural influence, became one of many cherished values, such as beauty and the glorious and heroic deeds of men. History entered into the curriculum since history glorifies man and his works.

Greek culture assumed prominence because people believed that both beauty and wisdom abided in the works of Plato. Thus, education in the Latin schools attempted to familiarize the young with the past and to lead them to desire a rich and full life. The works of Homer, Cicero, Virgil, and Quintilian grew to be dominant influences in the curriculum. Quintilian's *Ars Oratorio,* discovered by the humanist, Andrea Poggio, "in the cloister where it had lain hidden for several centuries" proved to be a stifling influence in human thought rather than a creative one. *Eloquentia* became the vogue. No phrase was to be used that was not found in the finest Roman letters of the time. "In this way they condemned their beloved Latin to change from a living language, which to a degree it had been in these Middle Ages, into a dead one."[6]

Though the Renaissance period produced memorable and ageless works of art, as well as artists and thinkers such as Leonardo Da Vinci, Michelangelo, and others whose thoughts and works have enriched the world for centuries, it made no comparable timeless impact on education. Understanding of the child and his developmental and educational needs moved slowly.

For instance, the famous and learned humanist, Maffeo Vegio, objected to cruel punishment for children, but harken to his alternative!

> If you are angry with your children and you hesitate to whip them flog your servants, a procedure which will frighten your own noble offspring.
>
> Another suggestion was to take them to executions . . . "to see a man hanging, bleeding or burning may have a wholesome effect on the moral development of a child."[7]

Comenius, John Locke, and Rousseau proved to be far more "human" as we shall see.

Comenius. A familiar and friendly name to students of educational history, Johan Amos Comenius (1592-1670) is an important name for students of children's literature, too. He was a sense preception learning theorist, and his *Orbis Pictis* takes primacy in the historical genesis of picture books for children.

Comenius combined ideas of mysticism with individualism which, in contrast to Luther and Calvin, had optimistic overtones. His ideas were more pantheistic in spirit. Though he believed that man and nature were one with God, there was less dualism in his philosophical statements. Rather, he viewed the phenomenological world with some empiricism as did Bacon. In his monumental work, *The Great Didactic,* he attempted to define causal relationships, but clear-cut analogies were impeded by the intermingling of mystic superstition with factual observation. His contribution to education, and to children's literature in particular, was his emphasis on the importance of teaching young people by using concrete objects, or by having pictures which explain and expand meanings of words in the text.

John Locke. A man of many talents, John Locke (1632-1704) was philosopher, physician, psychologist, statesman, and teacher. His writings seemed to attain the acceptable admixture of progressivism and conservatism for the tenor of the times.

---

[6]Ulich, *Educational Thought,* p. 112.
[7]Ibid., p. 112.

The populace was weary of religious wars and hatred. They sought more freedom and liberty from authoritarian political systems.

By this time, the old hereditary nobility had been augmented by the knights and members of the wealthy middle class who were more in sympathy with the new ideas which deviated from the position of absolutism and the divine right of kings.

Locke's practical ideas appealed to these English gentlemen who were ready to accept new ideas if some of the older and well-established mores remained inviolate.

It was a time of wanting to have one's cake and eat it, too. Half measures, rather than full servings of liberal ideas, was the mode. The limited monarchial powers of William and Mary made room for another constellation of power: aristocracy, men of wealth, and the High Church. A democracy of the privileged classes was the vogue.

Locke introduced the idea that an infant's mind is a "tabla rasa," a blank entity upon which experiences would be impressed. The kind of experiences which would develop fine English gentlemen were described in his *Some Thoughts Concerning Education* and other writings. He stressed the relationship between healthy physical development and healthy mental development. This started a trend in health books for children, and precepts on health began to take their place along with the precepts on manners and morals.

Because he perceived the mind as being maleable, Locke was a firm believer in good habit formation. He wanted to establish habits in the child which would lead to the development of reasoning power. In this Age of Wisdom, he adhered to the idea that man is a reasonable, rational creature if he is given the proper experiences to mold this reasoning power.

Fables were espoused by Locke as being excellent reading material. Here, as in other matters, Locke took a middle-of-the-road position. Being "enlightened" and "reasonable," he believed that children should read for pleasure. On the other hand, he did not wish to fill the child's head with "perfectly useless trumpery," and so he saw in the fable a vehicle in which children might find entertainment and delight but which would still offer food for the intellect.

> To this purpose I think *Aesop's Fables* the best, which being stories apt to delight and entertain a child may yet afford useful reflections to a grown man; and if his memory retain them all his life after, he will not repent to find them there, amongst his manly thoughts and serious business. If his Aesop has pictures in it, it will entertain him much the better, and encourage him to read when it carries the increase of knowledge with it; for such visible objects children hear talked of in vain, and without any satisfaction, whilst they have no ideas of them; those ideas being not to be had from sounds, but from the beings themselves, or their pictures. And, therefore, I think,

as soon as he begins to spell, as many pictures of animals should be got to him as can be found, with the printed names to them, which at the same time will invite him to read, and afford him matter of inquiry and knowledge. *Reynard, the Fox* is another book, I think, that may be made use of to the same purpose. And if those about him tell them it will, besides other advantages, add encouragement and delight to his reading, when he finds there is some use or pleasure in it. These baits seem wholly neglected in the ordinary method; and it is usually long before learners find any use or pleasure in reading, which may tempt them to it, and so take books only for fashionable amusements, or impertinent troubles, good for nothing.[8]

Though children were not released from lessons, morals, and precepts, Locke did inject a pleasurable aspect into children's reading and learning. To be sure, it was taking advantage of children to use pictures and entertaining fables as bait to impart the lessons and morals which were the true purposes of the reading. But it was a giant step forward—merely caring whether children were entertained or not, was significant.

It seems incredible and truly not comprehensible in our modern democratic frame of reference that an intelligent and enlightened man of John Locke's stature could write *Some Thoughts Concerning Education* to be implemented in the education of the upper classes, and in the same lifetime, write a treatise on "Proposals for the Bringing Up of the Children of Paupers."

It was his idea that all such children between the ages of three and fourteen should attend day "working schools" where learning a livelihood was the justification for providing bread and warm water-gruel to the "scholars." While Locke's conception was more akin to a technical or trade school, these "working schools" became instead the precursors of the deplorable workhouses.

> We do not suppose that children of three years old will be able at that age to get their livelihoods at the working school, but we are sure that what is necessary for their relief will more effectually have that use if it be distributed to them in bread at that school than if it be given to their fathers in money. What they have at home from their parents is seldom more than bread and water, and that, many of them, very scantily too. If therefore, care be taken that they have each of them their belly full of bread daily at school, they will be healthier and stronger than those who are bred otherwise. Nor will this practice cost the overseers any trouble; for a baker may be agreed with to furnish and bring into the school house every day the allowance of bread necessary for all the scholars that are there. And to this may be added, also without any trouble, in cold weather, as it be thought needful, a little warm water-gruel; for the same fire that warms the room may be made use of to boil a pot of it.[9]

---

[8]John Locke, cited in Adams, *About Books and Children*, p. 45.
[9]Ibid., p. 205.

It may be seen that Locke contained his humanism within the culturally conditioned attitudes of the aristocracy of which he was a member. Public (private) schools for "future gentlemen" were his concern.

Thus, the masses of children continued to have very little, if any, contact with books, while the upper-class children were finding reading a little more intriguing and pleasurable.

The Puritans. Despite the renaissance in art, music, and literature which brought renewed appreciation of the aesthetic in art forms, and despite the fact that, by mid-century, John Locke's philosophical statements of humanistic individualism were spreading, books for the majority of children remained dismally moralistic. The Puritans rejected the Neoplatonism of the Renaissance and fought a rearguard action against humanistic ideas. Since Locke addressed himself only to the upper classes and their children, Puritan ideas held sway among the middle and lower classes. Books for the majority of children of the seventeenth century in England and in the early American colonies fell into three categories—folk materials, books of manners and behavior, and religious books. Adults generally condemned the first, esteemed the second, and extolled the third.[10]

Religion held a pivotal position in the society of the time, particularly in middle-class England and America where the Puritan influence was such a dominant central force in the lives of the people. There was a singleness of purpose in the writing—the desire to awaken, to evangelize. The Puritan books addressed children for the same purposes as they addressed adults. The great reformers of the sixteenth century, Luther, Calvin, and Knox, sought to inspire individual initiative in men. Each man must seek to find his own salvation, to control his own destiny rather than blindly trust in God to mete out his fate. This emphasis on individualism in these times of humanistic thought, and the dissent and reformation in the established church took the form of extremism in the Puritan sect. Their lives became a concentrated and constant struggle against the forces of evil. Time was cherished. It was in the here and now that one must work for the salvation of one's soul.

The doctrine of original sin was inherent in this persuasion. Since man was considered to have been born evil, he must spend the rest of his life in atonement and in finding redemption. Children came to be considered as "little devils."

This gloomy notion of a child's origin came to be translated into a belief that children often were possessed by devils, evil spirits which had to be driven from the bodies of these unruly, un-adult-like children.

---

[10]William Sloane, *Children's Books in England and America in the Seventeenth Century* (New York: King's Crown Press, Columbia University Press, 1955), p. 8.

"I'll beat the devil out of you," was once a declaration of specific, literal intent.

> . . . The assumption in this doctrine is that if the adults succeeded in identifying and controlling the devil (wicked impulses) the young would become fine, moral adults.[11]

The "ultimate and laudable" aim in learning to read, according to the Protestant ethic in the seventeenth century, was to be able to read the Bible. Catechisms were the most widespread and numerous reading materials for children. Through the long and tedious sermons delivered at church, in catechisms, and in pious biographies, the child was brought to "remember his creator."

Some Puritans are purported to have given away printed catechisms from the Book of Common Prayer as they walked along the London streets, just as handbill advertisements are given out today. When one realizes how expensive printing was in those days, one can understand the fanaticism which possessed many Puritans in relation to "fostering the health of the child's soul."

Jean Jacques Rousseau. At a time when the major emphasis was on sharpening the muscles of the mind and filling it to the brim with all the knowledge in the world that it could absorb, Jean Jacques Rousseau's (1712-1778) exhortations to "retournez á la nature" had a strong impact on the complacency of educators of this period. Rousseau eschewed formal education for children until they attained the age of twelve. He believed that children should grow naturally, according to the free play of nature. In his *Émile,* he described growth and developmental stages. He stressed the importance of experiences being in harmony with physical and mental development. These stages were described as progressing from early sensory motor experiences, through the concrete learning period which he believed lasted until the eleventh year, when it gave way to a more intellectual conceptualization. He even believed that the child should not be required to learn to read until the age of eleven. These stages of intellectual development as postulated by Rousseau bear marked similarity to Piaget's modern theories of the epigenesis of the intellect. For the child's first book, Rousseau advised tutors to introduce *Robinson Crusoe,* since it was the story of an individual who had been reduced to a state of living with nature and of being dependent upon his own ideas and ingenuity to adapt to and cope with his environment.

Didactic stories written in the wake of his teachings stressed the idea of learning through experience. Many writers incorporated the idea of the preceptor—the adult authority who would reinforce behaviors and learnings which were in accord with this natural unfolding theory that

---

[11]Howard A. Lane and Mary Beauchamp, *Understanding Human Development* (Englewood Cliffs, N. J.: Prentice-Hall, 1959), p. 15.

Rousseau espoused. A stock literary character emerged in books for children—the all-wise and beneficent friend, teacher, or parent, who was constantly available to answer all questions propounded by the children in the books. The educational overtones incorporated into every experience served to make these books almost always dull.

> The blight which this deplorably figure has laid upon the work of the early nineteenth century is immense . . . His discourses run to paragraph after paragraph where one chosen sentence would have been enough for both the children in the story and the children who read it to have done with it.[12]

Mrs. Trimmer, Hannah More, and Thomas Day are among those whose works were permeated by "the everlasting wise person, the inevitable expounder of all pertinent facts."[13]

In the character of Sandford, in that popular book of the time, *The History of Sandford and Merton,* Thomas Day epitomizes Rousseau's *Émile.* Mr. Barlow, the tutor to the weak but wealthy Tommy Merton and his friend, the strong but less affluent Harry Sandford who saved Tommy from being bitten by a snake, becomes the omniscient character in this deploringly didactic saga. He exudes what his author-inventor believes is necessary and useful information, explaining and informing through *every* experience the two boys encounter.

In Maria Edgeworth's stories about Rosamond, "The Purple Jar" is a classic example of a narrative in which the child learns by experience. In this instance, the child learns through "bitter" experience. Poor Rosamond, who longed for the beautiful jar in the window and chose it, in spite of good advice, instead of the shoes she so sorely needed, learned to her great sorrow the ephemeral nature of her choice.

In spite of the fact that Rousseau's writings and educational philosophies were sharply criticized and that much of his philosophy, according to critics, contained only half-truths, in this time of decaying absolutism, his cry of "retournez á la nature" jolted the educational thought. His writing influenced educational methods, though many educators and parents experimented "unwisely and not too well" with Rousseauism. His respect for the harmony of nature and discipline had an impact on the thinking of those who were subsequently instrumental in shaping educational and psychological thought. He charted the course for looking at the human organism as one that grows gradually, from conception to maturity, through interaction with the environment in which it lives.

His impact on the attitude of parents toward children was forceful and unmistakable. Now children were looked upon as "little angels"

---

[12]Cornelia Meigs et al., *A Critical History of Children's Literature* (New York: Macmillan Co., 1953), pp. 97-8.
[13]Ibid., p. 98.

who could do no wrong. They were permitted to be children rather than "little adults." They became the center of the educational scene rather than satellites around the curriculum.

Comenius, John Locke, Rousseau, and others were the forerunners of modern concern for and study of the child as a growing organism with unique patterns of behaviors and needs. The emergence of the behavioral disciplines in modern times has presented new methods of studying human behavior. Researchers in the field of child growth and development have delineated ontogenetic stages of growth from conception through maturity. This knowledge of the biological development of the individual with its psychological concomitants has had tremendous impact on patterns and practices in child rearing in the home, in the school, and in the community. Children have a place in society which is uniquely their own. They are not viewed as miniature adults, devils, or angels, but rather as growing individuals whose behaviors and abilities are determined in large measure by the interaction of environmental and hereditary factors as they move along the growth continuum.

Teachers, parents, and librarians in modern times are aware that the preschool child is preoccupied with the task of acquiring language. His vocabulary is increasing at a fast clip. He may be observed rolling words around in his mouth, repeating and imitating rhymes and jingles and rhythmic syllables. Therefore, repetitional tales such as Wanda Gág's *Millions of Cats*, the fun and nonsense words of Seuss' stories, and the beautifully illustrated collections of Mother Goose verses are made available to him. Animals who are "himself in fur," like Frances in *Bedtime for Frances* and *Peter Rabbit* and *The Three Little Pigs* become his storybook friends. His ideas about his world are extended by books which help him attain concepts such as *Heavy Is a Hippopotamus*, (and it is, of course).

There is an awareness, too, of the primary school child as an active youngster whose overall physical growth is slowing down during this period of latency. Busily occupied in refining coordination in both large and small muscles, he is learning to read and to write. He is also extremely social and curious, interested in himself, his family, his friends, and in the environment which he encounters. He enjoys books which satisfy his curiosity about the world around him, such as Branley's *A Book of Astronauts for You*, stories of warm family relationships, such as *Evan's Corner* by Elizabeth Starr Hill, sheer fun and nonsense as found in Dr. Seuss' creations such as *To Think that I Saw It on Mulberry Street*, and of course, he enjoys the folk and fairy tales such as *The Lad Who Went to the North Wind*. It is fun for him to join in these flights of fancy, like waving a cloth to produce a mouth-watering meal. Though he knows it's only make-believe, this does not deter his enjoyment one whit.

The intermediate grade child in those years between nine and eleven, has his special growth patterns, interests, and reading needs, too. He becomes more interested in others and in the world around him. He is a staunch member of a peer group, a team, and a club. He tends to eschew the opposite sex, especially if he is a boy. He collects marbles, pictures, facts, and adventures. He is eager to find out all about everything, the moon, the stars, the earth, the oceans. Fanciful books such as *Miss Pickerel Goes to Mars, The Gammage Cup,* and *The Borrowers* permit him to let fancy stray with other "human beans," in a world which he knows is "make-believe." He enjoys larger than life-sized figures like *Paul Bunyan* and *Pecos Bill.* He also likes to read about fictional characters who could be real people—Henry Reed, or Homer Price. The biographies of great men are also available for his reading pleasure.

These children in the latter half of the twentieth century have a wealth of books from which to choose, and which meet their interests, needs, and abilities at all ages and stages of development. After nineteen hundred years of recorded time, children have achieved a place in society and a literature of their own.

QUESTIONS AND SUGGESTIONS

1. Identify some of the prevailing societal attitudes toward children from Caxton's time to the present. Discuss children's reading in relation to these attitudes.
2. Identify some of the cultural values in the United States in the twentieth century. Select from the vast array of children's books a few which seem to best reflect these values.
3. Choose several books which you believe to be appropriate for each age and stage of development: preschool, primary, middle and upper elementary years. In what way do your choices reflect the characteristics of these developmental stages?

SELECTED REFERENCES FOR CHILDREN

BOWMAN, JAMES CLOYD. *Pecos Bill.* Illustrated by Laura Bannon. Chicago: Albert Whitman & Co., 1937.

BRANLEY, FRANKLYN. *A Book of Astronauts for You.* Illustrated by Leonard Kessler. New York: Thomas Y. Crowell, 1963.

GÁG, WANDA. *Millions of Cats.* New York: Coward-McCann, 1938.

HAVILAND, VIRGINIA. *Favorite Fairy Tales Told in Norway.* Illustrated by Leonard Weisgard. Boston: Little, Brown & Co., 1961.

HILL, ELIZABETH STARR, *Evan's Corner.* Illustrated by Nancy Grossman. New York: Holt, Rinehart & Winston, 1966.

HOBAN, RUSSELL. *Bedtime for Frances.* New York: Harper & Row, 1960.

KENDALL, CAROL. *The Gammage Cup.* Illustrated by Erik Blegvad. New York: Harcourt, Brace & World, 1959.

MACGREGOR, ELLEN. *Miss Pickerel Goes to Mars*. Illustrated by Paul Galdone. New York: McGraw-Hill Book Co., 1951.

NORTON, MARY. *The Borrowers*. Illustrated by Beth and Joe Krush. New York: Harcourt, Brace & World, 1953.

✓SCHLEIN, MIRIAM. *Heavy Is a Hippopotamus*. Illustrated by Leonard Kessler. New York: William R. Scott, 1954.

SEUSS, DR. *And to Think that I Saw It on Mulberry Street*. New York: Vanguard Press, 1937.

SHEPHARD, ESTHER. *Paul Bunyan*. Illustrated by Rockwell Kent. New York: Harcourt, Brace & World, 1924.

SELECTED CHAPTER REFERENCES

ADAMS, BESS PORTER. *About Books and Children*. New York: Holt, Rinehart & Winston, 1953.

DAY, THOMAS. *The History of Sandford and Merton*. London: Lee and Shepard, 1875.

DEFOE, DANIEL. *Robinson Crusoe*. New York: Charles Scribner's Sons, 1920.

EDGEWORTH, MARIA. *Early Lessons: Rosamond, Frank, Harry and Lucy, etc.*, London: Routledge, 18–?.

FIELD, MRS. ELIZABETH M. *The Child and His Book*. London: Wells Gardner, 1891.

LANE, HOWARD, and BEAUCHAMP, MARY. *Understandinig Human Development*. Englewood Cliffs, N. J.: Prentice-Hall, 1959.

LOCKE, JOHN. *Some Thoughts Concerning Education*, with Introduction and Notes by R. H. Quick. New York: Macmillan Co., 1913.

MEIGS, CORNELIA; EATON, ANNE; NESBIT, ELIZABETH; and VIGUERS, RUTH HILL. *A Critical History of Children's Literature*. New York: Macmillan Co., 1953.

ROUSSEAU, JEAN JACQUES. *Émile: or, Education*. Translated by Barbara Foxley. New York: E. P. Dutton & Co., 1911.

SLOANE, WILLIAM. *Children's Books in England and America in the Seventeenth Century*. New York: King's Crown Press, Columbia University Press, 1955.

ULICH, ROBERT. *History of Educational Thought*. New York: Van Nostrand Reinhold Co., a division of Litton Educational Publishing, 1950, 1945.

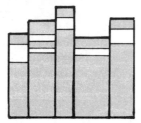

chapter 3

fantasy —
there were tales to tell

How far removed is the world of childhood! Its inhabitants seem of another species.

Tireless, full of the exuberance of life, from morning to night they run, shout, quarrel, make up and fall asleep only to begin again next day at sunrise. Their awkward young bodies are already imperious. Children are rich with all they do not own, rich with the potential wonders of their universe. Making believe is not only one of their earliest pleasures, it is their virtual spark, the token of their liberty. Reason does not curb them, for they have not yet learned its restraints. Happy beings, they live in the clouds, playing lightheartedly without a care.[1]

"Give Us Wings," the first chapter of Paul Hazard's inspiring book, is a plea for fantasy and "times of wondering" in literature for children. He deplores the obtuseness of adults who "want to suppress that happy interval of years in which we live without dragging the weight of life about us."[2] He continues,

They destroy those child landscapes that giants cover with great strides, where dwarfs crouch under the roots of the trees; those landscapes where the river talks with the fields that it bathes, and where the skies open to let a flock of fairies through.[3]

Children had giants, fairies, ogres, and dragons to their hearts' content in earlier times. In those days, adults and children alike enjoyed the same tales told at cottage firesides in humble dwellings. In castle halls, the affluent society might have listened to the wandering bards, the scops, the gleemen, or minstrels who, by any name, were both newsmen and entertainers of the times. These welcome travelers either recited heroic and poetic stories or sung them to the accompaniment of harp or lyre. Some of these sagas were learned from remote singers

[1]Paul Hazard, *Books, Children and Men* (Boston: Horn Book, 1944), pp. 1-2.
[2]Ibid., p. 4.
[3]Ibid., p. 5.

and tellers of tales. Others were the products of their own imaginations or were tales of wonder gleaned during their tours throughout the country.

These minstrels sang the heroic tales of heroes such as Cuchulain who slew the terrifying dog of Chulain. They told of Beowolf, too, who conquered the fierce monster, Grendel, later adding more glory unto himself by following Grendel's vengeful mother to the bottom of the sea and slaying her too! Ah, those wonderful heroes of old who could perform such fabulous deeds—Zeus who hurled resounding thunderbolts, and Apollo who drove across the sky in a flaming chariot.

If one were a humble peasant living in a cottage, he heard these epic tales and myths from friends who served meals in the lords' castles. These servants had an ear for music and good memories for words and plots. The tales served to ward off bogeymen and offered some security and comfort against the dark and unknown forces of nature. The peasants also listened to stories made up by a "spinner of yarns," the storyteller whose simple tales involved plain "folk" like themselves who, through bravery, trickery, resourcefulness, and boundless energy and endurance, accomplished amazing feats, thus winning for themselves wealth, jewels, princesses, and crowns, and the right to "live happily ever after."

These simple "rags to riches," anonymity and poverty, to fame and fortune type tales wherein tyrants are outwitted, and good conquers evil, are often called the "cottage" tales in English lore, or "haus" or "märchen" tales in German lore. They are thus distinguished from the heroic epics, legends, and ballads which were the court and castle literary fare.

It was long ago and far away when these myths, legends, fables, and tales were born. There were no books, no printing, no writing—at least not as we know it now—when these stories and tales were told and sung.

Myths

Today's young readers can explore in collections such as *The Golden Treasury of Myths and Legends* these myths created by men. The illustrations in this volume create the illusion of antiquity, seeming as they do to come directly from some ancient Grecian urn or from an Egyptian tomb. The tales are adapted by Anne Terry White from the world's great classics.

Here is the story of Daedalus, the renowned architect and sculptor of Athens. His overwhelming jealousy of Talus, his inventive nephew, led him to hurl Talus from the top of the Acropolis to his death. Filled with remorse and fear, Daedalus left Athens and wandered to King

Minos' Cretan kingdom. There, King Minos had a task for a master architect. It was to build a structure to house the Minotaur, that fearful monster with the head and shoulders of a bull and the legs and trunk of a man. What else but a labyrinth could provide a prison from which there could be no escape? Even Daedalus himself was nearly lost trying to find his way out. However, Daedalus was held prisoner in Crete because King Minos feared that the secret of the labyrinth would be revealed.

Daedalus envied the freedom of the birds as they flew across the sky. "Aha, why not fly away," thought he. He studied the secrets of a bird's flight, and then architect-sculptor-inventor that he was, he made feathered wings for himself and for Icarus, his son. But Icarus' buoyant spirits would not let him heed the warning:

> Be wise, not bold. Take a course midway between heaven and earth. For if you fly too high, the sun will scorch your feathers. And if you fly too low, the sea will wet them. Take me for your guide. Follow me and you will be safe.[4]

He flew too close to the sun, and so to his death.

Poor Daedalus, cursing his own skill and mourning his loss, believed that the gods had avenged his impulsive murder of Talus.

Another, and related, myth is that of Theseus, son of Ægeus, the king of Athens. When Theseus became a young man, he donned the embroidered sandals and the gold-hilted sword which his father had hidden under a large stone. This stone yielded to his strength on his eighteenth birthday. After this, he set out for Athens, slaying robbers and scoundrels as he went. At this time, the Athenians were in great mourning on account of the tribute which they were forced to pay to Minos, king of Crete. This tribute consisted of seven youths and seven maidens who were sent every nine years to be devoured by the Minotaur. Theseus volunteered, indeed demanded, to be one of these.

In Crete, Ariadne, daughter of Minos, became enamored of Theseus, and he returned her love. She gave him a sword with which to encounter the Minotaur, and a clue of thread by which he might find his way out of the labyrinth. With the aid of these, Theseus overcame the monster and escaped from the labyrinth. Unfortunately, in his excitement and joy to be sailing back to Athens, he forgot to exchange the black sails on the ship for white sails, a prearranged signal to his waiting father, of his son's victory. Poor Ægeus, in his grief at sight of the black sails, cast himself into the sea.

Tales of gods and heroes like these made up the mythology of the ancient world. Elements of the tales which defied understanding were given supernatural explanations. Though these hypotheses bore

---

[4]Anne Terry White, *The Golden Treasury of Myths and Legends.* Illustrated by Alice and Martin Provensen. (New York: Golden Press, 1959), p. 52.

no resemblance to cause and effect relationships in the natural world, they satisfied the wish for ordering the environment. Thus, a polytheism developed. In their attempt to give body to the mystic forces in the world, these early people created gods in their own image and likeness but who *were godlike* because of their great wisdom, beauty, and feats of wondrous power. These beings were also capable of jealousy, envy, anger, and other human frailties. Floods, tidal waves, droughts, blizzards, hurricanes, and typhoons were considered to be portents of an angry god or gods.

The Greek myths demonstrate the remarkable inventiveness of these ancient people who were also most observant. As they watched, they thought and then, like Archimedes, probably one of them said "Eureka," and a new god or a new constellation was born. Whatever had motion seemed to be alive in ancient Greek reasoning. They peopled the sky, rivers, seas, caves, grottos, mountain tops, and the earth's interior with immortal beings. They saw the big and the little bear, the giant, the lion, and other animals in the skies. Each star group or cluster, because it moved, took on the shape and form of an animal or a human being, for example, Sirius (the Dog Star) and the Pleiades (the sisters constellation).

The ancient Greeks also invented those lively, ethereal, and mysterious nymphs, dryads, and naiads rising from seas, gliding among trees, and floating across lakes and streams. Thus, the quite fearfully and threateningly mysterious unknown became peopled with friendly sprites and somewhat predictable gods who had human qualities like theirs, and who would watch over and protect them, but of whose wrath they must beware.

This is the way the myth was born. People in all times and all places build and weave their myths to explain the unexplainable, perhaps to try to attain the unattainable, or to give themselves courage to sustain what can be sustained—courage, fortitude, and the confidence to live fully.

The myths which have come down to us through the oral tradition demonstrate an evolution over the years in the way that they differ in kind and sophistication. The simplest, most straightforward myths are the "pourquoi" or "why" stories[5] which emerged in the first stages of mythmaking when the primitive people, like young children, asked the "why" questions repetitively. "Arachne," for example, is a simple tale which explains why the spider spins. Other tales evolved in an effort to explain the miracles of growth, weather, and seasons. Some sought to explain the origin of man and provide an answer for the question, "Where did I come from?" Kipling created the modern "pourquoi" with

_____

[5]May Hill Arbuthnot, *Children and Books* (Glenview, Ill.: Scott, Foresman & Co., 1964), p. 307.

his memorable stories that tell how the tiger got its tail and how the elephant got its trunk.

These simple "why" stories later became more allegorical in nature with somewhat complex symbolism. King Midas, known to most children today as he was to children in ancient Grecian times, still symbolizes stark and unadulterated greed. Allegorically, he is punished in a manner befitting this craven and niggardly person. In contrast, Philemon and Baucis are suitably rewarded for their welcoming kindness to those two weary travelers, Jupiter and Mercury. Thus is taught the allegorical lesson that humble service finds its own reward.

When the Romans invaded Greece, they not only occupied the land but they also usurped their gods, changing only the names. Zeus became Jupiter; Hera, the queen of the heavens became Juno; and so on. They built temples in the lands of their insatiable conquests, and by so doing, secured the "immortality" of their gods.

Germanic myths seem to be an adaptation of the Norse myths just as the Roman myths were adaptations of the Greek myths, but the names differ less. Odin in Norse mythology is the German god, Wodan; Sigurd and Brynhild became celebrated in Wagnerian opera as Siegfried and Brünhilde.

The stories of these mythological characters and creatures of ancient times have delighted generation upon generation of children. They have had a vivid picture of Phaeton who, enraged at being ridiculed by his schoolmates for his pretensions to heavenly paternity, seeks proof of his lineage. Their excitement has mounted high as they see Apollo, the sun god, grudgingly permit Phaeton to ride the heavenly chariot. And they somehow or other have accepted his sad ending, for who would or could dare to drive a fiery chariot across the sky? (Except astronauts?)

Man continues to build his myths. Since ancient times, he has wrested powers from the gods through "enlightenment" and use of "reason." As man continues to do as the ancients did—cope, adapt, and live in the earthly environment—he, too, must engage in flights of fancy which relieve the pressures and stress concomitant with the coping. He too must wish, dream, and aspire. He must revel in courage, bravery, heroic daring, and incredible accomplishment. In ancient times, man produced the pyramids and the Parthenon to prove his worth. In these modern times, man aimed for and attained the moon.

Epics

The Greek Iliad and Odyssey. Homer, a blind poet, is credited with being the composer of the epic poems, *The Iliad* and *The Odyssey.* According to legend, he wandered from city to city singing his songs some five or six hundred years before the birth of Christ. The exact place and time of Homer's birth remain veiled in mystery, though many Greek cities have laid claim to him. As was the case with Aesop, it cannot be clearly established whether Homer alone created and composed these masterpieces or whether he compiled stories which had been told to him.

The Iliad recounts the events of the Trojan war fought by the Greeks against King Priam of Troy to recapture Helen, the wife of King Menelaus of Greece. Through a variety of complex situations during the nine year siege of Troy, adventure and drama run high. The quarrel between Agamemnon and Achilles, with all its ramifications, over the spoils of the war makes stimulating reading.

The Odyssey is a long and exciting account of Ulysses' ten years of trials and adventures during his journey back to Greece from the Trojan wars. The Cyclops, the Lotus-eaters, Scylla, and Charybdis are familiar names to all who have experienced this ancient literary classic.

The English Beowulf. This, the oldest English folk epic, is believed to have been sung during the eighth century before the Saxons came to England. Beowulf, the dragon killer, has been immortalized in song and story. Prose and epic versions, as well as beautifully illustrated adaptations for children, continue to tell his dramatic story.

The Irish Cuchulain. A somewhat less familiar epic hero of Irish lore is Cuchulain who was known also as the "Hound of Ulster" because of his slaying a ferocious dog when he was a youth. The blood of the gods ran through his veins, and his amazing feats of strength are legend throughout Ireland and the world to this day.

The Scandinavian Sigurd. Another ancient hero is the Norseman, Sigurd. His feats of heroism and nobility, such as killing the dragon, Fafnir, and rescuing Brynhilde from a ring of fire, were the bases for the great German epic, "The Nibelungenlied," which was so gloriously set to music by Wagner.

The French Roland. The legendary hero who served Charlemagne has been immortalized in the French epic, "Chanson de Roland." Dating from the eleventh century, the epic includes many tales, among which is Roland's famous battle with the Saracens. His enchanted horn continues to summon readers just as, according to legend, it summoned Charlemagne to rescue him and his men from their mountain trap.

The Story of a "Knyghte Prisoner" and His "Morte d'Arthur." Knights, the Round Table, Camelot, and King Arthur were Sir Thomas Malory's literary gift to the English-speaking world. Malory, who was of Norman-English descent, was placed at an early age in the service of Richard de Beauchamp, Earl of Warwick, a descendant of the famed

Guy of Warwick. Young Thomas became imbued with the spirit of knighthood and all the glory and tragedy which made up the age of chivalry.

In England, Malory was accused of breaking into and robbing Coombe Abbey. For this deed, he was thrown into Newgate prison where he stayed throughout most of the remaining twenty years of his life. Whether Malory, with his band of one hundred rioters, was seeking forcible restitution for gross injustice and extortion, or whether, in those lawless times, he had indeed turned robber and thief, is not known.

He had received a fine education during his service with the scholar, Beauchamp. Because of this and his rank, he was allowed access to the books in the Grey Friars Library across the road. To pass the time, Malory began on a project of translating French romances into English. He became interested in the old Welsh hero tales which had been recorded in the continental romantic style. He developed a great reverence for Arthur and a kind of hero worship for Launcelot. He recounted the whole panoply of feudal chivalry with its dedication to God and to performing good deeds (but its unawareness of the fallacy and "ungodliness" of class systems and privileged society) with great simplicity and beauty. *Morte d'Arthur* was published in 1485 by William Caxton who was interested in bringing the French romantic literature to England and seized upon this work to introduce it to English readers.

Folk and Fairy Tales

"Sit down, Wanda-chen, and I'll tell you a märchen," and then Wanda Gág continues to tell us that,

> I settled down in my rocker, ready to abandon myself with the utmost credulity to whatever I might hear, everything was changed, exalted. A tingling, anything-may-happen feeling flowed over me, and I had the sensation of being about to bite into a big, juicy pear.[6]

Then came the beginning, perhaps this one, "In days of yore there lived a Queen. She was old and ugly, but her daughter, who of course was young and charming," which launched the tale of "The Six Servants" and the magic powers they used to break the enchantments of the Princess. It is one of Wanda Gág's delightful translations from Grimm.[7]

The Chinese child eagerly settles down as venerable grandmother beckons, "Let the children come nearer, and I will tell them the story

---

[6]Reprinted by permission of Coward-McCann, from *Tales from Grimm* by Wanda Gág. Copyright 1936 by Wanda Gág; renewed 1964 by Robert Janssen, p. vii.

[7]Ibid., p. 39.

of gentle 'Gwan Yin'," and with these words she might begin, "In earliest times, my little ones, there lived an Emperor whose name was Po Chia. With his Empress he ruled the land wisely and well." Thus the children are embarked upon the tale of that gentle goddess of mercy whose name means "she who hears prayers." This is one of the surefire spellbinders included in *Tales of a Chinese Grandmother,* so carefully selected by Frances Carpenter from various sources of Chinese mythology, and sensitively illustrated by Malthe Hasselriis. The young reader or listener is indeed transported right into a Chinese inner courtyard behind the two halves of "the bright red gate in the gray wall where Lao Lao, the Old One, came each day to tell her tales."[8]

The children of Norway hear "Once upon a time, there was an old widow who had one son," heralding the story of "The Lad and the North Wind." Or it might be "Once upon a time—but it was a long, long time ago—there were two brothers. One of them was rich, and one was poor," as off the Norwegian storyteller goes into the "pourquoi" tale of "Why the Sea Is Salt." Both of these stories are retold by Virginia Haviland in *Favorite Fairy Tales Told in Norway* and are accompanied by Leonard Weisgard's illustrations which so charmingly transport the reader to Norway.[9]

"A long time ago there lived a king whose wisdom was celebrated far and wide" is the opener for "The White Snake," in which the young servant lad, after tasting the White Snake, was given the magical power to converse with birds and animals. "There was once a man and his wife who had long wished in vain for a child," introduces that well loved familiar tale, "Rapunzel." "There was once a poor widow who lived alone in her hut with her two children. They were called Snow-White and Rose-Red because they were like the flowers that bloomed on two rosebushes which grew in front of the cottage." And "There was once an old nanny-goat," or "Once upon a time, there was a girl who was lazy and a miller who was very poor," and so on. These are opening phrases of the stories collected so diligently and indefatigably by the Brothers Grimm.[10] These beginnings are the signals which portend wonder and excitement to come for the young children who so fortunately continue to share in the folklore of the ages.

Whether it be in French, English, Dutch, African, German, or Chinese, here is the literature which children have unfailingly chosen and staunchly kept throughout the ages, though not without a struggle

---

[8]Frances Carpenter, *Tales of a Chinese Grandmother.* Illustrated by Malthe Hasselriis. (New York: Doubleday & Co., 1937), p. 29.

[9]Virginia Haviland, *Favorite Fairy Tales Told in Norway.* Illustrated by Leonard Weisgard. (Boston: Little, Brown & Co., 1961), p. 67 and p. 30.

[10]Jacob and Wilhelm Grimm, *Grimm's Fairy Tales.* Mrs. E. V. Lucas, Lucy Crane, and Marian Edwardes, trans., Fritz Kredel, illus. (New York: Grosset & Dunlap, 1945.)

during the seventeenth and eighteenth centuries. Then the "mental pabulum of Godly children" were the Bible and other religious and moral fare.[11] But why were the children (and adults in earlier days) so inflexible, persistent, and insistent in clinging to these tales throughout the ages?

What claim do these tales have to immortality?

They have been defined as all forms of narrative which have been handed down through the years and which eventually have been preserved in written form. They are tales of wonder and delight, of magic and bravery, and of all the qualities of human strength and weakness which are the bone, muscle, marrow, and nerve centers of our being. They are a legacy of anonymous oral traditions in which reside the "accumulated wisdom and art of simple everyday folk"[12] from time immemorial. They are stories in which evil may prevail over good for a while but in which love in all of its "goodly" and "godly" manifestations of kindness, charity, and purity of heart prevails triumphantly over whatever wickedness and evil may be besetting the protagonist of the tale. Children, and adults, too, may trust that the plot of the folktale will eventually bring about a satisfactory solution to the troubles, sorrows, and trials of the "good people," the hero or heroine of the story.

Folktales, lasting as they did through many centuries of telling and retelling, were honed down throughout the ages so that they now have a parsimony of language and a restrained style which permits the reader or listener to fill in details as he wills. The language, typically rhythmic and flowing, is the product of the melodic and mellifluous voices and tempos of one after another fine storyteller throughout time. Sentences and plot sequences are unencumbered by the excess verbiage often linked with explanatory and descriptive phrases. These tales have a dignity and simplicity which are the hallmark of great literature.

Young children have especially enjoyed the simple accumulative and repetitional tales such as "The Old Woman and Her Pig," and "The Gingerbread Boy." These have the thinnest thread of a plot but maximal rhythm rising to a lovely crescendo which signals the start of the swift and gay downward spiral.

> the cat began to eat the rat
> the rat began to gnaw the rope
> the rope began to hang the butcher
> the butcher began to kill the ox
> the ox began to drink the water
> the water began to quench the fire

---

[11]Monica Kiefer, *American Children through Their Books, 1700-1835* (Philadelphia: University of Pennsylvania Press, 1948.)
[12]Arbuthnot, *Children and Books*, p. 263.

the fire began to burn the stick
the stick began to beat the dog
the dog began to bite the pig[13]

and naturally, piggy jumped over the style, (wouldn't you?) and the little old lady got home that night. These stories probably originated in the ancient chants, or ritualistic games and rites of the primitive peoples.

It is interesting and significant to note the variety in type, style, theme, and motif found in this vast wealth of literature. The talking beast tales are about animals who talk among themselves or with human beings. Among the favorites of children are the inimitable "Puss in Boots" who wandered in and out of chapbooks with all of his guile and persuasion; "Aansi," another shrewd and sly one, who originally hailed from West Africa; those groups of "threes," goats and pigs; and the ugly beast whom "Beauty" finally released from the wicked spell. These rank among the immortals in literature and memory.

Noodles, drolls, sillies, and numbskulls tickled the funny bones of the ancients as well as of present-day people, both young and old. These morons of folklore seem to be more lovable than our modern ones, though surely they were just as obtuse. Whether they be called Lazy Jack or Epaminondas, Mr. Vinegar or Gudbrand,—no matter from what country they hailed—one thing they held in common was their incredible inability to relate cause and effect. If they had, of course, there would not have been all those hundreds, thousands, millions and billions of hours of fun and gaiety which these charming and gullible souls have provided for hundreds, thousands . . . etc. of children over centuries of time.

Romance was rife throughout the ages, too. In the folktale, it was remote and idealistic. Plots were concerned with the plights of the hero or heroine and with the feats of strength, cunning, and courage that were performed to mitigate the situation. Heroes accomplished the impossible to win the hand of the princess. They rescued her from the tower prison, or they released her from the wicked stepmother and a life of drudgery, or they freed her from some evil curse or from other tyrannical and untenable predicaments in which she was trapped. "The prince won the hand of the maiden," "they were married and lived happily ever after," and "if you travel there you may see them to this day in their beautiful golden palace by the sea," were apparently satisfying endings for the folk throughout the ages, and they satisfy the young reader and listener today. It is the event and the action which keep him enthralled, and he has faith that honesty, perseverance, pa-

---

[13]Cited in May Hill Arbuthnot, *Arbuthnot Anthology of Children's Literature,* rev. ed. (Glenview, Ill.: Scott, Foresman & Co., 1961), p. 8. Reprinted by permission of G. P. Putnam's Sons.

tience, strength, courage, and humility will win out in the end, that all will be right in the story world and in his own world, as well.

May Hill Arbuthnot reminds us that it is the "magic" that is at the heart of folktales.

> These are the stories that justify the children's name for the whole group—"fairy tales." Fairy godmothers, giants, water nixies, a noble prince turned into a polar bear, the North Wind giving a poor boy magic gifts to make good the loss of his precious meal, three impossible tasks to be performed, a lad searching for the Water of Life— these are some of the motifs and some of the fairy people that give the folktales a quality so unearthly and so beautiful that they come close to poetry.[14]

The French had their *Fairie* world. Old Celtic tales had their "wee" people. German tales had their dwarfs and trolls who often lived underground. The Greeks had their nymphs, nixies, and dryads. These supernatural creatures were sometimes young and lively, sometimes old and wizened. Sometimes they were dwarfs like Rumpelstiltskin, or trolls like the one under the famed bridge which the "Three Billy Goats Gruff" trod so many times. Perhaps they were elves who helped poor shoemakers and maidens in distress. All were part of the magic and enchantment of the tales.

Differences in ethnic origins are apparent to students of folklore, but children who enjoy the tales care not so much about from where they came, as they do about what these magic people or objects do. Will it be benevolent or will it be harmful? What is going to happen? The folktale often contains acts of cruelty and horror, but it does not play upon the details of these incidents. It happens indeed, but

> No blood drips from the Raven's sister's hand when she cuts off a finger, not an "ouch" escapes her lips. The wolf is cut open so the six kids can escape, and the mother goat sews the stones into his stomach without any suggestion that the wolf is being hurt. Children accept these stories as they are—symbolic interpretations of life in an imaginary land of another time.[15]

Children are quite secure in their faith that all will be right eventually even before they hear the familiar phrase which signals the ending, "and that was the way it was," or "snick! snack! snout! my story is out!"

Values which seem to be universal are firmly interwoven and imbedded in the tales. The power of love over cruelty is repeatedly underscored. Acts of mercy, charity, humility, patience, fortitude, and courage are always rewarded; acts which violate these virtues are punished.

---

[14]Arbuthnot, *Children and Books*, p. 272.
[15]Charlotte Huck and Doris Young Kuhn, *Children's Literature in the Elementary School* (New York: Holt, Rinehart & Winston, 1968), p. 169.

Wishes for comfort and security are expressed over and over—a good husband, a loving wife, fine food, clothes, homes, and personal possessions are the sure benefits of virtuous living. So for many, "here in the fairy tale is the world as it ought to be—sometimes ruthless of necessity, but sound at the core."[16]

This vast wealth of fanciful literature preserved in the oral tradition down through the ages, though not originally belonging to children, has been commandeered by them and presently comprises a rich heritage and source of children's literary experience.

But it was not always this way. There was a break in the long sequence of folk and fairy tale sharing and enjoyment. For a while, it was farewell to these stories of rollicking action and mighty deeds, and to these supernatural creatures with magic powers who roamed above the world or who dwelled in mysterious underground caves. Alas, they were frowned upon as being unsuitable and too frivolous by the Puritan who was so intent upon the hereafter that he made the present a grim and mirthless time for himself and his children.

Virtue was considered by the Puritans to have its own reward, but other attributes like tolerance, charity, and mercy were not evident in this religious persuasion. This "War with the Devil" did not permit any "allurements of the world" such as "little histories" and fairy tales.

> Most godly children pursuing the path of virtue began with the Bible and read it in its usual form from cover to cover. Less valiant souls pursued the juvenile versions, reduced to the tender capacities of little Readers . . . so as under God to make those excellent Books take such a firm hold of the young minds . . . as no Accidents of their future lives will ever blot out.[17]

"The struggle against man's innate depravity reached epic proportions during the seventeenth century."[18] The ballads and tales were considered wanton and ungodly and had to go underground. Since prohibition often tends to strengthen the desire for what is banned, the chapbooks became the "literary speakeasies" of the seventeenth and eighteenth centuries. The stories which children and adults loved so well were printed and reprinted in these rudely contrived books which sold for only a few pence. During the first half of the seventeenth century, shortened forms of the old tales and stories were often issued in ballads and broadsides.

These broadsides were sheets approximately twelve by eighteen inches, usually printed on only one side. After being read and reread, they often became decorations for nursery walls.

---

[16]Arbuthnot, *Children and Books*, p. 282.
[17]Kiefer, *American Children . . . Books*, p. 29, 30.
[18]Ibid., p. 30.

As early as 1593, a ballad version of the story of the babes in the woods, was entered in the Stationers' Register as "The Norfolk Gentleman, his Will and Testament, and how he committed the keeping of his children to his own brother, who dealt most wickedly with them, and how God plagued him for it."[19] This tragic saga turns up again in chapbook form in Ashton's collection.[20]

The most Lamentable and Deplorable

HISTORY

OF THE

Two Children in the Wood:

CONTAINING

The happy Loves and Lives of their **Parents,** the Treachery and barbarous Villany of **their** Unkle, the duel between the Murdering **Ruffians,** and the unhappy and deplorable death of **the** two innocent Children.

    As also an Account of the Justice **of God** that overtook the Unnatural Unkle; **and of the** deserved Death of the two murdering **Ruffians.**

TO WHICH IS ANNEX'D

THE OLD SONG UPON THE SAME

LONDON : PRINTED BY AND FOR W.O., AND SOLD BY THE BOOK
SELLERS.

Title page of "Two Children in the Woods." From *Chap-Books of the Eighteenth Century* by John Ashton. Printed by permission of Benjamin Blom, Inc.

What spine-tingling thrillers these chapmen had in their packs as they visited fairs, markets, cottages, and castles seeking out customers. As soon as books were made available at cheap prices, the chapmen carried them with ribbons, laces, gewgaws, patent medicines, and all the "trumpery," as Autolycus, the immortal rogue, admits.

---

[19]William Sloane, *Children's Books in England and America in the Seventeenth Century* (New York: King's Crown Press, Columbia University Press, 1955), pp. 70-71.
    [20]John Ashton, *Chap-Books of the Eighteenth Century* (New York: Benjamin Blom, 1882), p. 370.

As he traveled the countryside of Shakespeare's time, the chapman hawked ballads about

> How a usurer's wife was brought to bed of twenty-money-bags at a burden, and how she longed to eat adder's heads, and toads carbonadoed;
> . . . of a fish that appeared upon the coast, on Wednesday and fourscore of April, forty thousand fathom above water, and sung this ballad against the heart of maids.[21]

Sloane, in his chapter, "Farewell, Rewards and Fairies," identifies the early eighteenth century as the period when folktales and fairy tales began to be thought of as the exclusive property of children. It was at this time that Isaac Bickerstaffe (Richard Steele) wrote with some amusement of his godson's interest in the old romantic tales.

"Jack the Giant-Killer," "Dick Whittington," and "Tom Thumb" were among the popular fare. In the introduction to his fascinating collection of chapbooks, John Ashton speaks with some nostalgia about these "relics of a happily past age . . . when these little chapbooks were nearly the only 'mental pabulum' offered."[22]

After the Restoration, and the passing of the Licensing Act which sanctioned censorship and prohibited the erection of printing presses except in London, Oxford, and Cambridge, (from 1662-1669, and again from 1685-1692 when it was rigidly enforced), the chapmen flourished, since no printing was allowed and, therefore, no books were available in the provinces except those that these "running stationers" brought.[23]

The running peddlers of the eighteenth century carried extensive wares. Most of the chapbooks in Ashton's collection were printed by William and Cleur Dicey whose establishment was originally at No. 4 Aldemary Churchyard and later was removed to Bow Churchyard. The name was later changed to C. Dicey, and from this house, according to Ashton, nearly all of the original chapbooks were published. He has appended a list of 120 publications.

Chapbooks dealt with a variety of content—religious, diabolical, supernatural, superstitious, romantic, humorous, legendary, historical, biographical, and criminal. Many of these stories, legends, and biographies were called "histories," as may be seen by titles such as "The History of Sir Richard Whittington," "The Famous and Renowned History of Guy, Earl of Warwick," "The History of the King and the Cobbler," and so forth. The chapbook version of the famous History

---

[21]Ashton, *Chap-Books*, p. vi.
[22]Ibid., p. v.
[23]Sloane, *Children's Books*, p. 72.

of Tom Thumb, wherein are declared *His Marvelous Acts of Manhood Full of Wonder and Merriment,* starts like this:

> In Arthur's court Tom Thumb did live
>   A man of mickle might
> Who was the best of the table round
>   And eke a worthy knight.
>
> In stature just an inch in height
>   Or quarter of a span
> How think you that this valiant knight
>   Was proved a valiant man.[24]

Tom Thumb being carried by a raven. From *Chap-Books of the Eighteenth Century* by John Ashton. Printed by permission of Benjamin Blom, Inc.

Tom Thumb as a knight on horseback. From *Chap-Books of the Eighteenth Century* by John Ashton. Printed by permission of Benjamin Blom, Inc.

It continues through page after page of situations such as his falling into the pudding, being carried away to a giant's castle by a raven, being taken out to sea by a large fish, arriving at King Arthur's court, and so on until his demise.

The chapbook version of Tom Thumb is interspersed with prose. It had been taken from the original ballad printed in 1630 for John Wright. As has been noted, this little hero is found in folklore throughout the world, but British tradition holds that he died at Lincoln, a town in England populated with Danes. He is mentioned in Sir Walter Scott's "Discoverie of Witchcraft" where he is classed as "the puckle, hobgobblin, Tom Tumbler boneless and such other bugs."[25]

[24]Ashton, *Chap-Books,* p. 208.
[25]Ibid., p. 206.

Another Tom of chapbook fame is Thomas Hickathrift who also had a "famous history." He was the Samson of his time, with the strength to pull up a tree and carry it as though it were a twig, and with the strength to kill the giant "with no more mercy upon him than a bear upon a dog," and to cut off his head "after which he went into the cave and there found great store of gold and silver which made his heart leap for joy." After thwarting highwaymen and warding off disasters, and after building a fine home, he finally met his match in the nimble Tinker to whom he yielded after some reeling blows. Tom apparently was able to take his comeuppance in good grace, for he took the Tinker home where the story leaves them "curing their bruises."[26]

Tom Hickathrift carrying a tree. From *Chap-Books of the Eighteenth Century* by John Ashton. Printed by permission of Benjamin Blom, Inc.

Tom Hickathrift slaying a giant. From *Chap Books of the Eighteenth Century* by John Ashton. Printed by permission of Benjamin Blom, Inc.

---

[26]Ibid., pp. 192-203.

Of course, Jack, the hero of all heroes, was to be found in the chapbooks—*The Pleasant and Delightful History of Jack and the Giants.*[27]

Title pages of the first and second parts of *Jack and the Giants.* From *Chap-Books of the Eighteenth Century* by John Ashton. Printed by permission of Benjamin Blom, Inc.

Jack has been a perennial favorite of children. Does the reader remember how, with a pickax and a shovel, he dug a pit twenty-two feet deep, and after covering it over, he blew his horn? And how the sound of the horn, of course, brought the giant, Cormoran, running out, only to fall into the pit where Jack killed him with the ax? And there was the time that crafty Jack tricked the two-headed giant of Flintshire:

> Soon after the Giant went to breakfast on a great bowl of hasty pudding, giving Jack but little quantity; who being loath to let him know he could not eat with him got a leather bag, putting it artfully under his coat, into which he put his pudding, telling the Giant he would show him the trick; so taking a large knife he ripped open the bag which the Giant thought to be his belly, and out came the hasty pudding; which the Welsh Giant seeing, cried out, Cot's plut, hur can do that hurself; and taking up the knife he ripped open his belly from top to bottom and out dropped his tripes and trulibubs so that he immediately fell down dead.[28]

After slaughtering many more giants with his wiles, need it be said that he married a duke's daughter upon freeing her from the giant Galligantus' enchanted castle?

[27]Ibid., pp. 184-191.
[28]Ibid., pp. 189-190.

What joyous fare for the children who had only a few adult books and the Bible to read before the advent of the chapbooks.

These stories of a romantic nature were among the most popular with children. The humorous stories were prime favorites then, too, as they are now. The Three Wise Men of Gotham were unbelievably obtuse and hilarious:

> On a time the Men of Gotham fain would have pinned in the Cuckow, that she might sing all year; all in the midst of the town they had a hedge made round in compass, and got a cuckow, and put her into it and said, Sing here, and you shall lack neither meat nor drink all the year—The Cuckow when she perceived herself encompassed within the hedge, flew away. A vengence on her, said these Wise Men, we made not the hedge high enough.[29]

Title page of the *Merry Tales of the Wise Men of Gotham*. From *Chap-Books of the Eighteenth Century* by John Ashton. Printed by permission of Benjamin Blom, Inc.

It appears that there were chapbooks to please everyone—humorous, romantic, superstitious, and so forth. Many of these stories were adapted and abridged from the original. The style and language were often distorted in the process. The illustrations were crude, and the printing and paper were of the most inexpensive kind. But for the first time in history, books were made available at a very nominal sum, and it was possible for children and adults of the lower classes to collect a sizable library.

---

[29]Ibid., p. 278.

Many of the children's favorite tales were not primarily intended for children. In the original chapbook versions, the humor is often very broad, and sometimes it would be considered in poor taste to present them as reading fare for children today.

From the time of Caxton, romances and fairly tales were not considered by many to be appropriate reading for young children. There was little fiction, except the surviving medieval romances, until about 1550. As the rediscovered classics began to make their appearance and as the new culture of the humanists infiltrated the upper classes, the old stories were considered to be fit fare only for the non-aristocratic classes and for children. It was, perhaps, the impact of scientific and rational thought in the seventeenth century as well as the decrease of illiteracy resulting from the appearance of more vernacular schools which finally relegated the fairies and other supernatural beings into the realm of childhood.

In England and France, simple fairy stories and folktales, told in unaffected manner by governesses or nursemaids, had been the favorite bed time stories for generations, but it was the Comtesse d'Aulnoy who is credited with having introduced the telling of fairy stories to the salon gatherings in France. She thus started the fashion which eventually led to their being set down in written form. The salons were made up of wits, writers, and philosophers of the day. The characters and backgrounds of the tales as told in the salons were in the sophisticated versions and, in most respects, belonged only superficially to fairyland.

As nursery tales, they were told in simpler form by nursemaids or governesses. Since young children do not probe for motives or symbols in their stories, it was the exciting, active plot, and the sympathetic or wicked characters and magical happenings which enthralled them.

Perrault. There was one person on the French scene at the time who actually chose to record the fairy tales in the simpler nursery form and wrote eight of them in that never-to-be-forgotten volume, *Contes de Ma Mère L'Oye.* Academic questions continue to arise as to whether it was the eminent scholar, Charles Perrault, or whether it was his son, Pierre Perrault d'Armancour, who authored this first collection of eight tales. This volume became the progenitor of those later collections by the Brothers Grimm and others in which the folklore of the ages is stored. The most notable and fortunate circumstance in the recording of the tales is that "neither the contents of the stories nor their simple phraseology were seriously tampered with in publication."[30] The Perrault tales preserved the simplicity which was the result of the years of polishing which the stories had undergone in their telling until the remaining

---

[30]Percy Muir, *English Children's Books: 1600-1900* (New York: Frederick A. Praeger, Publishers, 1954), p. 39.

tale was quite perfect in its style and form. Paul Hazard exalts the telling of these tales:

> Perrault is as fresh as the dawn. We never reach the end of his accomplishments. He is full of mischief, humor and charming dexterity. He never seems to be achieving a tour de force, lifting a weight, looking for applause, but he seems to be having more fun than anyone, relating these prodigious stories entirely for his own pleasure. From time to time he appears to say a word, starts up a dialogue, then quickly withdraws realizing that of all faults, indiscretion is the clumsiest. These characters should act by themselves, he is only there to do their will, to record their conversation.[31]

The Brothers Grimm. Perrault was the initial raconteur of fairy tales in written form. They were translated into English in 1729. Children had to wait almost a hundred years for the next great collection of their historical heritage of folk and fairy tales. And of course, it was none other than the Brothers Grimm who came forth to do the task. They are credited with having been the originators of the modern science of folklore. While studying law, Jacob became interested in early German literature through a collection of folk songs edited by Ludwig von Armin and Clemens Brentano. This led to a study of folktales, and Jacob and his brother, Wilhelm, embarked upon a career which gave those *Grimm's Fairy Tales* to the world forevermore. The tales first appeared in 1812 and were entitled *The Kinder and Hausmärchen Tales* which translates to *Nursery and Household Tales*. The Edgar Taylor translation in English, 1823-26, was entitled *German Popular Stories.* These were illustrated by George Cruikshank, and from the day of publication to the present time, most English-speaking children count Rumpelstiltskin, Snow White and the Seven Dwarfs, Hansel and Gretel, and a host of other characters as first-name acquaintances.

The Grimms were painstaking about their sources and forebore tampering with the language or the plots which they wrote verbatim as they heard them from the lips of old storytellers whom they sought out in all parts of the realm. Though the stories have become the true favorites of young people, the brothers did not have children in mind when they started their work. They were university professors—philologists—and in the beginning, their interest in all forms of traditional literature was secondary to their interest in the roots and development of the German language. It is told that they were so meticulous about "recording the tales exactly as the people told them, writing down every variant separately, . . . that they avoided their publisher friend, Brentano, whose predilections for 'touching up' they well knew. The Grimms were determined that the language of the people should get into print exactly as it was, and it did."[32]

---

[31]Hazard, *Books, Children, Men,* p. 9.
[32]Arbuthnot, *Children and Books,* p. 259.

Asbjörnsen and Moe. The Norwegian folklore was recorded by a zoologist, Peter Christian Asbjörnsen, and a poet and theologian, Jörgen E. Moe. Like the brothers Grimm, they gathered the native tales of their country directly from the old storytellers who had learned them from storytellers, and so on, back into time. Asbjörnsen combined his search for folklore with his zoological field expeditions. Both projects were amenable to the need for traveling into remote areas. In the more isolated sections, he was able to find, not only specimens and interesting terrain, but communities that still relied on the art of the storyteller for entertainment.

Moe traveled on his holidays, seeking out the tale-tellers with great success and recording them with the utmost skill, veracity, and sensitivity. The *Norwegian Folk Tales* was the culmination of this devoted search and faithful recording.

Though the mood of most folktales, except for the drolls, tends to be somewhat serious, the Nordic collections of Asbjörnsen and Moe possess more optimism and humor. "Henny Penny," for instance, is extremely amusing as she creates a disaster area from a simple happening—an acorn falling upon her head. The mischievous and nimble "Pancake" is sheer fun, too.

There are no gauzy-winged fairies in these tales, but trolls, hags, and witches abound, and there is magic enough for everyone in fiddles, tablecloths, sticks, and other simple items. What could be more enchanting than the polar bear prince whose spell is so excitingly broken in "East o' the Sun and West o' the Moon"?

Sir George Webbe Dasent's name is almost inextricably intertwined with Asbjörnsen and Moe's collections. An Englishman of remarkable talents, he was diplomat, journalist, and linguist. While on a diplomatic assignment in Stockholm, he became interested in the tales. He was primarily interested in the Icelandic language. Among his works are the *Grammar of the Icelandic* and a translation of the *Prose or Younger Edda*. In 1859, his brilliant translation of *Popular Tales from the North* joined the growing library of folktale classics in English and became the basis for all future translations in English. He was able to capture the folk flavor and idioms with unerring accuracy.

"Boots and His Brothers" incorporates the simplicity of these tales with magical happenings which somehow seem quite reasonable. It begins, of course, "Once upon a time, there was a man who had three sons," (not two or four, but that folktale number, "three"), "Peter, Paul, and John." John was Boots because he was the youngest. The King, whose palace was not too far from the cottage where they lived, wanted a tree felled and a well dug. Now these tasks do not seem to be insurmountable, but the oak tree was "so stout and big, it took away all of the light from the palace," and since the king's palace was "high, high up on a hill," it meant that solid rock must be penetrated to dig the well. But the three brothers were willing to try, especially since the reward was marriage to the king's daughter.

> They hadn't gone far before they came to a fir wood, and . . . they heard something hewing and hacking away upon the hill among the trees.
> "I wonder now what it is that is hewing away up yonder," said Boots.
> "You're always so clever with your wonderings," said his brothers both at once. "What wonder is it, pray, that a woodcutter should stand and hack on a hillside?"
> "Still, I'd like to see what it is, after all," said Boots; and up he went.
> "Oh, if you're such a child, 'twill do you good to go and take a lesson," bawled out his brothers after him. . .

Boots found the magic ax, spade, and walnut and returned to his brothers. As was to be expected, when they reached the palace, the two brothers failed at the task.

> Now Boots was to try. . . .
> "Hew away!" said he to his ax.
> Away it hewed, making the chips fly, so that it wasn't long before down came the oak. . . .
> "Dig away!" said he to his spade.
> The spade began to dig and delve. . . .
> Then, Boots took out his walnut and laid it in one corner of the well. He pulled out the plug of moss.
> "Trickle and run!" said Boots.
> The nut trickled and ran, till the water gushed out of the hole in a stream. . . .
> Now Boots had felled the oak which shaded the King's palace and dug a well in the palace yard; so he got the Princess and half the kingdom, as the King had said.
> Then Peter and Paul had to say, "Well, after all, Boots wasn't so much out of his mind when he took to wondering."[33]

And the brothers point out the simple lesson imbedded in the tale. It's *good* to wonder about things!

Joseph Jacobs. The recorder for British and Celtic lore was Joseph Jacobs. His was a mission to bring joy to children. It was not uppermost in his mind that his contribution be scholarly. Because his chief concern was to provide children with these well-loved tales, he took the liberty of deleting certain brutal and coarse episodes and passages. He also took liberties with the dialect so as to make it readable and understandable to the young English audience. He used the sources of other collectors: Kennedy, Celtic; Halliwell, English; and Chambers, Scottish.

---

[33]Slightly adapted in the *Arbuthnot Anthology*, p. 77. From *Popular Tales from the Norse*, by permission of G. P. Putnam's Sons.

Jacobs had an unerring touch in selection and adaptation of tales for his collections. He knew what boys and girls would enjoy. *English Fairy Tales* and *More English Fairy Tales*, (1894), are representative of typical qualities of the English folktale. They are humorous but rarely romantic. In that the tales are almost matter-of-fact, Jacobs seems to have captured the spirit of England.

An excerpt from Tom Tit Tot demonstrates the English flavor of the tales.

> "A-why," says he, "I was out a-hunting today, and I got away to a place in the wood I'd never seen before. And there was an old chalk-pit. And I heard a kind of a sort of humming. So I got off my hobby, and I went right quiet to the pit, and I looked down. Well, what should there be but the funniest little black thing you ever set eyes on. And what was that doing, but that had a little spinning-wheel, and that was spinning wonderful fast, and twirling that's tail."[34]

Paul Hazard summarizes:

> Fairy tales are like beautiful mirrors of water, so deep and crystal clear. In their depth we sense the mystery of experience of a thousand years. . . .
> . . . See how every child repeats, through the tales, the history of our species and takes up anew the journey of our spirit from its beginnings. Threats, pursuits, mountains that cannot be climbed, rivers that cannot be crossed, all this dream material is found again in the fabulous stories that please children. Like themselves in the life that they begin and to which they return as soon as they fall asleep, their favorite heroes soar, glide, fly, cover seven leagues at one stride. The impossible and the possible mingle. . . . And this chaos, far from astonishing a child reader, seems natural to him as if he remembered passing through it himself twenty thousand years ago.[35]

Fables

Aesop. In 1484, Caxton gave *Aesop's Fables* to the English-speaking world. These stories, possibly from ancient Egyptian and Oriental sources, were gathered up by a German named Stainhowel in the fifteenth century and translated into French by Jules Machault, a monk at Lyons. From this work, Caxton translated into the English, and "Voila! It was read to pieces," according to Percy Muir in his *English Children's Books*, since only one perfect and two imperfect copies survive.

---

[34]Joseph Jacobs, ed. *English Fairy Tales* (New York: G. P. Putnam's Sons, n.d.).
[35]Hazard, *Books, Children, Men*, p. 157.

Aesop's fables have been a challenge and an inspiration to illustrators as have the Mother Goose rhymes. Their printing history may be recorded through the succession of illustrators with whose names the publications are linked. Their simplicity in both action and actors make them extremely adaptable to illustration.

Fables are essentially little lessons. A situation is set up in which a character or characters, always flat presentations, do just one thing. Sometimes the moral is stated. Sometimes it is left for the reader to do his own abstracting. The reader, of course, is supposed to emulate the sage lesson or beware of the folly which is portrayed. The raconteur determines the particular moral. Throughout the centuries, the lessons of Aesop have run the gamut of worldliness and cynicism to strict morality. In various tellings, the same fable has been given completely different interpretations. In one version of "The Fox and the Grapes," the fox's labeling the inaccessible grapes "green" has had a "sour grapes" connotation. Caxton's translation, and his interpretation, are quite the opposite.

> A fox looked and beheld the grapes that grew upon a huge vine, the which grapes he much desired for to eat them. And when he saw that none he might get, he turned his sorrow into joy, and said, "These grapes are sour, and if I had some I would not eat them."
>
> He is wise which faineth not to desire the thing the which he may not have.[36]

Aesop, whose name has been synonymous with fable to all literate people, is believed to have been a Phrygian slave in the sixth century B.C. Most historians report that he was a hunchback and a mute but that the gift of speech was bestowed upon him by the goddess, Isis, to whom he had unwavering devotion. Because he was adept at creating these fables and fabulous situations wherein the masters came off a very second best, his talents were rewarded. He was freed and was made an advisor to the king. But, in the manner of the ancient legends, this prosperous state didn't last. He was accused of theft, falsely, of course, and came to a violent demise. He was executed by being thrown from a cliff.

Who really knows? But all indications point to the fact that some ancient person possessed unusual ability as a storyteller. A collection of Aesop's Fables was made by Demetrius Phalereus in the fourth century B.C. Fables appear that predate Aesop, and so it seems likely that some of his fables were simply a retelling of older ones; but some, perhaps, were his own innovations.[37]

---

[36]*Aesop: Five Centuries of Illustrated Fables,* selected by John J. McKendry (New York: The Metropolitan Museum of Art, 1964), p. 12.

[37]Ibid., p. 6.

The Panchatantra Tales. The Panchatantra, meaning "five books," are tales of Kashmir, with possible origin about 200 B.C. Another name which is linked to them is "The Fables of Bidpai." These collections are found in a variety of linguistic translations among which are Persian, Latin, and Arabic.

The Panchatantra tales are much longer than the Aesop fables. Stories are created within stories. Their purpose is to teach a wise conduct of life, and so philosophical verses are interwoven with the thread of the story. The majority of the Panchatantra tales are for adult reading, but Maude Dutton's collection, *The Tortoise and the Geese and Other Fables of Bidpai*, contains thirty-four stories, illustrated by E. Boyd Smith, which children enjoy.

THE PARTRIDGE AND THE CROW

A Crow flying across a road saw a partridge strutting along the ground.

"What a beautiful gait that Partridge has!" said the Crow. "I must try to see if I can walk like him."

She alighted behind the Partridge and tried for a long time to learn to strut. At last the Partridge turned around and asked the Crow what she was about.

"Do not be angry with me," replied the Crow. "I have never seen a bird who walks as beautifully as you can, and I am trying to learn to walk like you."

"Foolish bird!" responded the Partridge. "You are a Crow, and should walk like a Crow. You would look silly indeed if you were to strut like a partridge."

But the Crow went on trying to learn to strut, until finally she had forgotten her own gait, and she never learned that of the Partridge.[38]

The Jataka Tales. Perhaps the oldest as well as the largest body of fables is that group which comes from ancient Buddhist sacred literature. Originally written in Pali, a dialect of Sanskrit, their time of origin, like all of these old fables, is not definitely known. Carvings depicting Jataka beasts, carvings that had been made as early as the second century B.C. have been unearthed. Jataka, a Buddhist name for story, depicts Buddha reincarnated as various animals—a lion, a deer, and so forth. The lesson evolves from the observations made.

An example may be seen in the story, "The Turtle Who Couldn't Stop Talking." The turtle had been offered a ride by two young geese . . .

"Now take the middle of (this stick) in your mouth, and don't say a word until we reach home," they said.

---

[38]Maude Barrows Dutton, "The Partridge and the Crow" from *The Tortoise and the Geese and Other Fables of Bidpai* (Boston: Houghton Mifflin Co., 1936), p. 231.

The Geese then sprang into the air, with the Turtle between them, holding fast to the stick.

The village children saw the two Geese flying along with the Turtle and cried out: "Oh, see the Turtle up in the air! Look at the Geese carrying a turtle by a stick. Did you ever see anything more ridiculous in your life!"

The Turtle looked down and began to say, "Well, and if my friends carry me, what business is that of yours?" when he let go, and fell dead at the feet of the children."[39]

La Fontaine. "Le fablier," (the fable teller) was none other than Jean de La Fontaine, (1621-1695), poet, member of the Royal Academy, and a contemporary of Charles Perrault.

In 1668, he dedicated his first collection of fables to the six-year-old Dauphin of France. Because La Fontaine was a skilled poet, the fables are in verse form, easy to read and pleasing to the ear. Forests and meadows, perhaps patterned after the Champagne countryside of his childhood, are the settings for his marvelous birds and beasts and their fable encounters. Many of these stories are probably drawn from Bidpai and Aesop sources. Brevity and the single striking episode are characteristic of the La Fontaine fables. However, the lovely French verse loses its flavor in translation, and so these fables, in English, are written in prose.

The Fox and the Crow

Mister Crow sat on the limb of a tree with a big piece of cheese in his mouth.

Old Mister Fox smelled the cheese from a long way off. And he came to the foot of the tree and spoke to the crow.

"Good morning, Mr. Coal Black Crow,
How beautiful and shining your feathers grow,
Black as the night and bright as the sun,
If you sing as well, your fortune is won."

At these words Mr. Crow joyously opened his beak to sing his creaky old crow song.

And the cheese fell down to the ground. The fox snapped it up in his mouth.

As he ran away he called back over his bushy tail, "My dear Mr. Crow, learn from this how every flatterer lives at the expense of anybody who will listen to him. This lesson is well worth the loss of the cheese to you."[40]

In fables such as these were imbedded universal truths in one brief, dramatic incident using few characters, typically animals.

---

[39]Ellen C. Babbitt, retold by, *Jataka Tales,* Animal Stories. Ellsworth Young, illus. (New York: Meredith Corp., 1912. Reprinted by permission of Appleton-Century-Crofts, 1940).

[40]Margaret Wise Brown, adapt. *The Fables of La Fontaine* (New York: Harper & Brothers, 1940).

Who could resist these sage observations on the foibles of human nature or the wonder of the fairy tale, the simple directness of the folktale people or the glamour, panoply, and drama of the myths, legends, and epics? But resistance there was. During the Puritan period, they were considered "worldly and immoral" and were thought to be "impractical and frivolous" during the didactic age.

Fanciful Literature for Children

Resistance to this vast array of fanciful literature finally weakened after Perrault, the Grimm brothers, Hans Christian Andersen, and others broke down the barriers. By mid-nineteenth century, fanciful literature was popular and approved reading for children.

The most cherished threesome in the whole world for some people— "The Three Bears"—was created, it is said, by Robert Southey, and published in his *Doctor* (1834-1837). Scholars do not reach consensus as to whether Southey created or retold this favorite. But a smashing success it was, finding its secure place with the other memorable animal triads, "The Three Little Pigs" and "The Three Billy Goats Gruff."

Hans Christian Andersen. The "ugly duckling," Hans Christian Andersen, (1805-1875), is the first person to author a group of fairy tales rather than to collect them. In 1835, after writing his novel, *The Improvisator,* which met with success, he wrote four fairy tales for children, "The Tinder Box," "Big Claus and Little Claus," "The Princess on the Pea," and "Little Ida's Flowers." These were followed in a separate volume by "Thumbelina," "The Naughty Boy," and "The Traveling Companion." "The Daisy" and "The Dauntless Tin Soldier" came soon after. They appealed to young and old, even though entitled *Wonder Stories for Children.* "The Ugly Duckling," (purportedly symbolizing Andersen's life—from early deprivation and loneliness to a gracious, secure, and elevated position), "The Nightingale," "The Wild Swans," and others contain depths of meaning which the more mature reader abstracts.

Mary Howitt's translations of Andersen's tales into English were published in 1846. They have been prime favorites with children for 120 plus years and show no indication of declining favor.

Andrew Lang. Another well-received and well-loved group of fairy stories were those of Andrew Lang, a highly respected and scholarly Scottish folklorist. Lang believed that the oral traditional literature was originally derived from events and experiences in human life, and that it was built around the beliefs, rituals, and observances which were universally experienced. Out of his vast study and search for traditional stories, he created the "Color" fairy books, blue, red, green, and yellow,

(1889-1894). Both old and modern tales were incorporated in these volumes. Though Lang was criticized by some folklorists for his adaptations, children have continued to enjoy Aladdin, Dick Whittington, Cinderella, and a host of others as they read *The Blue Fairy Book* and the other color fairy books.

Charles Kingsley. *The Water Babies* was published by Charles Kingsley in 1863. Though somewhat laden with preaching and moralizing, this book, which he wrote for his youngest son, Grenville, portrays his deep love for children. It is fanciful and humorous as it tells the story of the little chimney sweep who turned into a water baby. Kingsley's knowledge of nature—the ways of trees, insects, rocks, and tides— is interwoven with his clergyman's beliefs about life and religion into adventures which made enjoyable reading in the 1860's and which continue to be enjoyed in the 1960's and 1970's.

Lewis Carroll. During the second half of the nineteenth century, college professors as well as clergymen were thinking about children's entertainment through literature along with their education. On a memorable July afternoon, when an Oxford don, Charles Dodgson, took the three daughters of Dean Liddell on a rowing excursion, he entertained them (and children and adults from that day forward) with some of the most remarkable and enjoyable fanciful stories that have ever been concocted. Alice Liddell's Christmas greeting from Mr. Dodgson was

John Tenniel: A Mad Tea-Party, from *Alice's Adventures in Wonderland* by Lewis Carroll. Reproduced by permission of The Horn Book, Inc.

a manuscript of those stories, written by hand and illustrated by him. This version of the stories, accompanied by those perfect Tenniel drawings, was published in 1865 by the Macmillan Company. The rest is literary history—*Alice in Wonderland* and *Through the Looking-Glass* are truly a heritage of creative writing which all children and adults may share.

Kenneth Grahame. Toady, Ratty, Mole, and Badger made their appearance in the first decade of the twentieth century, along with Peter Rabbit. What a fruitful time for children's reading this was.

Kenneth Grahame's son, Alastair, was being sent to the seashore for the summer, but he was reluctant to part with his father who told wonderful bedtime stories about Toad and his friends. Alastair, or "Mouse" as he was nicknamed by his fond parents, extracted a promise from his father to mail the stories to him in serial form so that they could be read every night in installments. Subsequently, since *Everybody's Magazine* was anxious to publish something written by Grahame, Mrs. Grahame suggested that the letters be submitted. A manuscript called *The Wind in the Reeds* was sent to *Everybody's*. Incredible as it may seem from the perspective of a half century later, *Everybody's* turned it down because it was not thought to meet the quality of Grahame's two former publications, *The Golden Age* and *Dream Days*. Some time later (1908), it was published as *The Wind in the Willows* by Methuen and Company in London and by Scribner's in New York. It achieved instant and lasting success. An interesting note is that the editor of *Everybody's* did eventually recover from his trauma when he realized his gross error in judgment, and he later named his country home "Toad Hall" in honor of Kenneth Grahame's great contribution to the literary joy of children and adults throughout the world.

Beatrix Potter. Once upon a time there were four little rabbits, and their names were Flopsy, Mopsy, Cottontail, and Peter. Everybody knows about mischievous Peter and his excursions into Mr. McGregor's cabbage patch. Beatrix Potter did for the very young children in 1902 what Kenneth Grahame did for the older children in 1908. Both authors made animals in children's own images and likenesses, (themselves in fur), to be enjoyed while the child remains young, and to provide him with warm memories throughout his life.

Rudyard Kipling. A writer who proved himself to be master of the pourquoi form was Rudyard Kipling. The *Just So Stories* with their exquisite language—"In the high and far off time, Oh Best Beloved"—transport children back in time to the beginning of beginnings. Kipling's wit, wisdom, and humor were combined exquisitely to produce incomparable modern fantasy in the year 1912.

Wanda Gág. "Hundreds of cats, thousands of cats, millions and billions and trillions of cats" were created with such grace, rhythm, and apparent ease by Wanda Gág in her modern fanciful story, *Millions of Cats,* that it has retained classic status from the time of its publication in 1925 despite the wealth of fine modern fanciful literature published in the intervening years.

And so this literary heritage of myths, legends, epics, folk and fairy tales, and fables have been told and retold, collected, adapted, and published. They are available in exciting and colorful volumes which permit boys and girls today to enjoy this vast array of folklore as did their ancestors.

The wealth of traditional literature is steadily augmented by modern fanciful stories. Lloyd Alexander, for example, writes a tale of castles and magic, *The Castle at Llyr*, in the manner of olden tales. Virginia Kahl's *The Duchess Bakes a Cake* is folktale humor of the highest quality. Marcia Brown faithfully adapts the credulity of the townspeople in *Stone Soup*, as she does the ethereal beauty of *Cinderella*. Emmy Payne's *Katy No-Pocket* is a talking animal tale of pure artistry, and "Chanticleer" returns to the barnyard in full panoply in Barbara Cooney's treatment of the old tale, *Chanticleer and the Fox*. The above are a mere "licking of the spoon," which is part of the preparation for the fine feast of fancy, wonder, and joy—a child's literary pleasure and "treasure for the taking."

Literary experiences with fancy, both traditional and modern, may serve as the vent and release for pent-up emotions and stresses. They also offer a "time of wondering" and delight where imagination and fancy may roam in unfettered, unshackled time and space. In this regenerative manner, child and man keeps his creative genius alive so that he may continue to dream "the impossible dream."

QUESTIONS AND SUGGESTIONS

1. How did the minstrels, bards, scops, and storytellers of earlier times contribute to the field of children's literature?
2. Compare folktales of various ethnic origins which have similar plots and themes. Observe differences in style, characters, and incidents.
3. Select a traditional myth, legend, folktale, and fable. Compare them with selections from modern fanciful literature of each type. How are they similar? How are they different?
4. What modern publications might be considered similar to chapbooks? Discuss these similarities. What are the major differences?

SELECTED CHAPTER REFERENCES

ANDERSEN, HANS CHRISTIAN. *Fairy Tales*. Translated by Mrs. Edgar Lucas. Everyman's Library. New York: E. P. Dutton & Co., 1953.

ARBUTHNOT, MAY HILL. *Arbuthnot Anthology of Children's Literature*. Glenview, Ill.: Scott, Foresman & Co., 1961.

———. *Children and Books*. Glenview, Ill.: Scott, Foresman & Co., 1964.

ASBJÖRNSEN, P. C., and MOE, JÖRGEN E. *Norwegian Folk Tales*. New York: Viking Press, 1938.

ASHTON, JOHN. *Chap-Books of the Eighteenth Century*. New York: Benjamin Blom, 1882.

BABBITT, ELLEN C., retold by. *Jataka Tales, Animal Stories*. Illustrated by Ellsworth Young. New York: Meredith Corp., 1912; Appleton-Century-Crofts, 1940.

BROWN, MARGARET WISE, adapter. *The Fables of La Fontaine*. New York: Harper & Brothers, 1940.

CARPENTER, FRANCES. *Tales of a Chinese Grandmother*. Illustrated by Malthe Hasselriis. New York: Doubleday & Co., 1937.

DUTTON, MAUDE BARROWS. "The Partridge and the Crow" from *The Tortoise and the Geese and Other Fables of Bidpai*. Boston: Houghton Mifflin Co., 1936.

GÁG, WANDA. *Tales from Grimm*. Translated and illustrated by Wanda Gág. New York: Coward-McCann, 1936.

GRIMM, JACOB and WILHELM. *Grimm's Fairy Tales*. Translated by Mrs. E. V. Lucas, Lucy Crane, and Marian Edwardes. New York: Grosset & Dunlap, 1945.

HAVILAND, VIRGINIA. *Favorite Fairy Tales Told in Norway*. Illustrated by Leonard Weisgard. Boston: Little, Brown & Co., 1961.

HAZARD, PAUL. *Books, Children and Men*. Boston: Horn Book, 1944.

HUCK, CHARLOTTE, and KUHN, DORIS YOUNG. *Children's Literature in the Elementary School*. New York: Holt, Rinehart & Winston, 1968.

JACOBS, JOSEPH, ed. *English Fairy Tales*. New York: C. P. Putnam's Sons, n.d.

KIEFER, MONICA. *American Children through Their Books, 1700-1835*. Philadelphia: University of Pennsylvania Press, 1948.

McKENDRY, JOHN J., sel. *Aesop, Five Centuries of Illustrated Fables*. New York: The Metropolitan Museum of Art, 1964.

MUIR, PERCY. *English Children's Books: 1600-1900*. New York: Frederick A. Praeger, Publishers, 1954.

SLOANE, WILLIAM. *Children's Books in England and America in the Seventeenth Century*. New York: King's Crown Press, Columbia University Press, 1955.

WHITE, ANNE TERRY. *The Golden Treasury of Myths and Legends*. Illustrated by Alice and Martin Provensen. New York: Golden Press, 1959.

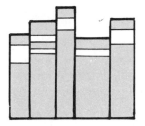

chapter 4

poetry —
there were songs to sing

Rhymes and Jingles

Children for unknown periods in time—in how many countries or how many ages we do not know—have had the pleasure of listening to, saying, and singing rhymes and jingles. These have been variously christened nursery rhymes, songs, jingles, melodies, and lullabies. Crying babies have been lulled throughout the years by the singing or chanting of these rhymes. Toddlers have been entertained, amused, or diverted as loving adults have played "Patty-Cake, Patty-Cake Baker's Man" with hands; "This Little Piggy Went to Market" with toes; or "Ride a Cock Horse to Banbury Cross" on a bouncing and jouncing adult foot. Children loved them, learned them, and joyously repeated them.

The second volume of Tommy Thumb's *Pretty Song Book*, probably printed about 1744, seems to be the earliest published collection of nursery rhymes, at least the earliest one which has survived.* It contains eleven rhymes still familiar today: Great A, little a, Bouncing B; Ride a Cock Horse (not in its modern form first found in Gammer Gurton's Garland); Baa, Baa, Black Sheep; Cock Robin; Hickory Dickory Dock; Ladybird, Ladybird; There was a little man and he had a little gun; Mary, Mary, Quite Contrary; Oranges and Lemons; Little Tommy Tucker; and Sing a Song of Sixpence. This book was a miniature, measuring about three and a quarter by one and a quarter inches. Small type and small woodcuts were used.

Perhaps the earliest rhyme recorded in a book written for children is "A was an Archer."

---

*As nearly as the historians can tell, there never was a first volume of the song book. Only Volume II survives today, and there is no record to be found anywhere of a Volume I. This matter is the subject of several pages in John Newbery's *A Little Pretty Pocket-Book*.

Concomitant with the rising interest in the science of folklore was the development of a serious interest in nursery rhymes and nursery tales. Research revealed that many of the rhymes and jingles appeared to be of incredible antiquity, some of them probably originating in the chants and rituals of the very primitive people. In many of the well-known and repeated nursery jingles, there are shadowy traces of folklore which suggest their possible ancient origin.[1]

In the United States, these rhymes and jingles of varying origins in time and place are commonly grouped together as *Mother Goose Verses*. These old chants and ditties were probably passed on by word of mouth for generations before they were gathered together and recorded in collections.

Scholars and historians of Mother Goose have delved into the origins of these well-known and loved rhymes in search of answers to the "who," "what," and "when," questions concerning Mother Goose. It appears that these have remained moot questions for the most part. Had "The Real Mother Goose" been asked to stand up in a quiz game during the eighteenth century, several contenders from several countries might have risen.

One of the earliest known uses of the name was in 1697 in France when Perrault's *Contes de Ma Mère L'Oye* (Tales of Mother Goose) was published. This was a collection of eight familiar folktales, including *Puss in Boots, Cinderella,* and *Little Red Riding Hood.* They were translated into English in 1729.

Whether the name had appeared in print before 1697 cannot be established. But on the frontispiece, the woman spinning away at her loom surrounded by a boy, a girl, a man, and a cat absorbed in her contes is designated as "ma mère L'Oye." She might have been the governess of Charles Perrault and also of his son. Another explanation was that the tales were named for Goose-footed Bertha who may have been the wife of Pepin and mother of Charlemagne, or else the wife of Robert II of France (970-1031). Both of these Berthas purportedly told stories to children of the court, the while spinning or working on intricate tapestries. There seems to be as much uncertainty surrounding the origin of the name "Mother Goose" as there is concerning the authorship of *Contes de Ma Mère L'Oye*—whether they were in fact written by Charles Perrault, or whether his eldest son, Charles Perrault d'Armancour, was the original recorder of these tales.

In the old Granary Burying Ground in the heart of Boston, one may spy Mother Goose's tombstone. What more proof do we seek, the reader may ask! According to scholarly research, Dame Goose's collec-

---

[1]Katherine Elwes Thomas, *The Real Personages of Mother Goose* (New York: William Morrow & Co., 1930), p. 8.

tion of nursery rhymes, entitled *Songs for the Nursery; or Mother Goose's Melodies,* was published in Boston by her son-in-law, Thomas Fleet, in 1719. No copy of this printing has ever been found. It is believed by most students to be a legendary tale, but who really knows? There *was* a Dame Goose, and she *did* live and die in Boston. Her daughter, Elizabeth, married Thomas Fleet, a printer and publisher on June 8, 1715. The ceremony was performed by no less a personage than the famed Cotton Mather. These facts are documented. But whether or not Thomas Fleet of Pudding Lane, Boston, did indeed publish a volume called *Mother Goose's Melodies* in 1719, antedating Newbery's publication by more than forty years, can only remain in the realm of speculation.

And so, the contenders are a goose-footed Queen Bertha of France in the eighth century, or one in the eleventh century, Perrault's governess in the seventeenth, and Dame Goose of Boston in the eighteenth century. Will the *real* Mother Goose please stand up!!!

John Newbery, with the aid of Oliver Goldsmith, it is reported, used the title, *Mother Goose's Melody or Sonnets for the Cradle,* in a compilation published in 1760 and 1765. Part I contains many of the old favorites sung by mothers and nurses "calculated to amuse children and excite them to sleep." Part II contains "those of the sweet songster and Muse of Wit and Humour, Master William Shakespeare, Embellished with Notes and Maxims, Historical, Philosophical and Critical."[2]

Arbuthnot suggests that later research raises questions as to whether Newbery in truth published this volume, whether it was his stepson, T. Carnan, who advertised it in the *London Chronicle* for January 2, 1781, or whether it was Francis Powers, Newbery's grandson, who published it for threepence in 1791 from No. 65 St. Paul's Churchyard.[3]

And so whether it was with the aid of Goldsmith or without him, whether it was Newbery, his stepson, or his grandson, Mother Goose, whoever she may have been, has been here over the centuries and is here to stay. Apparently, she is, as Cornelia Meigs testifies, "an indestructible treasure of the human race."[4]

Around the year 1784, *Gammer Gurton's Garland* by Joseph Ritson was published. This book contained There Was an Old Woman Who Lived in a Shoe; Bye Baby Bunting; Ride a Cock Horse; Hark, Hark, the Dogs Do Bark; Goose, Goosey Gander; A Diller, a Dollar; and Come Let's to Bed, Says Sleepy Head. The *Garland* of 1810 contained 136

---

[2]Bess Porter Adams, *About Books and Children* (New York: Holt, Rinehart & Winston, 1953), p. 138.
[3]May Hill Arbuthnot, *Children and Books* (Glenview, Ill.: Scott, Foresman & Co., 1964), p. 79.
[4]Cornelia Meigs et al., *A Critical History of Children's Literature* (New York: Macmillan Co., 1953), p. 153.

rhymes and included such well-known ones as Litle Bo-peep, Old Chairs to Mend, Humpty Dumpty, I Love Sixpence, and Jolly Little Sixpence.[5]

Two valuable New England editions of Mother Goose were published early in the nineteenth century. One was *Mother Goose's Quarto or Melodies Complete,* published in 1824, by Monroe and Francis. It contained forty-eight of the Newbery rhymes and many from Gammer Gurton's Garland. A very similar edition, with a foreword by Edward Everett Hale, appeared in 1833.[6]

Here we find Ma'am Goose herself addressing her "dear little blossoms" on the opening pages. We see an old crone talking to small children. She is projecting her irritation toward those who would abolish nursery rhymes in favor of couplets of manners and morals. Listen as she blasts her critics:

> Fudge! I tell you that all their batterings can't deface my beauties, nor their wise pratings equal my wiser prattlings; and all imitators of my refreshing songs might as well write a new Billy Shakespeare as another Mother Goose—we two great poets were born together, and we shall go out of the world together.
> No, no, my Melodies will never die,
> While nurses sing, or babies cry.[7]

The origin of the rhymes and their meanings has also been the subject of much scholarly research in both England and America. Katherine Elwes Thomas' long and painstaking research involved examination of rare volumes in the Bodleian Library at Oxford, the British Museum Library at London, the Public Libraries of Bristol, and the Library of Congress, Washington, D. C.; it included perusal of state papers and forgotten memoirs of the famous personages who, it was believed, were being lampooned in these verses; and it necessitated much travel throughout sections of England and Scotland—sections which were the settings for some of the jingles.

> The result of this fascinating work has been the establishing beyond all controversy that the nursery rhymes, largely of Jacobite origin, are political diatribes, religious philippics, and popular street songs, embodying comedies, tragedies, and love episodes of many great historical personages, lavishly interspersed with English and Scotch folklore flung out with dramatic abandon.[8]

Though Miss Thomas' research led her to have strong faith in her findings, Iona and Peter Opie, in their scholarly research which resulted in The Oxford Dictionary of Nursery Rhymes, found that the theories

---

[5]Percy Muir, *English Children's Books: 1600-1900* (New York: Frederick A. Praeger, Publishers, 1954), p. 77.
[6]Adams, *About Books and Children,* pp. 139-140.
[7]Arbuthnot, *Children and Books,* p. 77.
[8]Thomas, *Real Personages of Mother Goose,* p. 17.

concerning the origins and meanings of the rhymes were so numerous and varied that they tended to cancel one another out.

> The story of "Sing a song of sixpence," for instance, has been described as alluding to the choirs of Tudor monasteries, the printing of the English Bible, the malpractices of the Romish clergy, and the infinite workings of the solar system. The baby rocked on a tree top has been recognized as the Egyptian child, Horus, the Old Pretender, and a New England Red Indian.[9]

Many historians agree that probably some of the rhymes were in fact political satires, since freedom of speech to criticize those in power was not permitted. Such comments were considered treasonous, and so they were camouflaged in nonsense verse.

It appears that "Little Miss Muffet" may have been Mary, Queen of Scots, and that the spider was John Knox who was demanding that she recant her Catholicism. Frighten her he did, but she was staunch in her faith and never recanted.

Miss Thomas offers detailed documentation to show that Jack Horner, a gentleman's son in the neighborhood of Glastonbury was made the bearer of twelve title deeds of churchly estates to the king. These were placed in a pie, as was the delivery custom of the day. It is recorded that Jack did in fact filch one of these deeds by tearing the crust open wide enough to pull out the deed to the Mills Park estate which is held by his descendants to the present time.

Lampoons, riddles, chants, lullabies, incantations, prayer-rhymes, and rhyming formulas all seem to be incorporated in these verses. "Thirty Days Hath September," "Multiplication Is Vexation," and "Crosspatch, Draw the Latch" were known in the sixteenth century or earlier. The game of Bo-Peep was played as early as 1364. People were singing "Three Blind Mice" in 1609 if they had access to the music book *Deuteromelia*, and Jack Sprat and his wife were licking the platter clean in 1639. Some mythological origins have been suggested, for instance, that Jack and Jill might be a jingle describing the waxing and waning of the moon. It seems probable that "Rain, Rain Go Away" and other rhymes of this nature may have originated in the folklore as chanting charms.

Scholars continue to search for more authentic data concerning the origins of this vast collection of rhymes while generation after generation of children continue to clap, dance, play, spin, and sing to their compelling and lively rhythm, not really caring from where they came —caring only that here they are!

9Iona and Peter Opie, eds., *The Oxford Dictionary of Nursery Rhymes* (Oxford: The Clarendon Press, 1951), p. 27.

Manners and Morals in Poetry

"Some Excellent Verses for the Education of Youth," a collection
of early verse for children as the title suggests, published in 1708,
primarily contained admonitions in accordance with the prevailing
attitudes that anything written for children must be for the purpose of
improving their manners and morals.

Many writers of juvenile poetry in the eighteenth century and in
the early years of the nineteenth century approached their task with
the same staunchness of purpose as did that "monstrous regiment" of
didactic writers, Mrs. Barbauld, Mrs. Trimmer, the Kilners, and others.
(See Chapter 5, pp. 84-91.) The cultivation of morals and manners and
the acquisition of useful knowledge was uppermost in the thoughts of
these sincere but misguided writers of the times.

Eliza Lee Follen (1787-1860).   One of these was an English verse
writer, Eliza Lee Follen, who set herself to deleting the nonsense from
Mother Goose. Such temerity must be admired, though the idea is
horrifying and appalling. No wonder Mother Goose was in such a fret
as she addressed her "dear little blossoms."

In the preface to her miniature book called *Little Songs for Little
Boys and Girls,* Mrs. Follen succinctly states the prevailing attitudes of
the times.

> It has been my object . . . to catch something of that good humored
> pleasantry, that musical nonsense which makes Mother Goose so at-
> tractive to children of all ages. Indeed, I should not have thought of
> preparing a collection of new baby songs . . . if I had met with
> another book of this kind adapted to the capacity, taste, and moral
> sense of children, so I have attempted to imitate its beauties, and
> what is a far easier thing, to avoid the defects of Mother Goose
> melodies.

An example of Mrs. Follen's adaptations follows. Here is the
original:

> One misty, moisty morning
> When cloudy was the weather,
> I chanced to meet an old man
> Clothed all in leather.
>
> He began to compliment
> And I began to grin—
> 'How do you do?' and 'How do you do?'
> And 'How do you do?' again!

and now Mrs. Follen's work:

> The poor man is weak,
> How pale is his cheek!

> Perhaps he has met with some sorrow;
> Let us give him a bed,
> Where his poor weary head
> May rest, and feel better tomorrow.[10]

How could she do this to those beautiful words, "misty, moisty, morning," which immediately enclose one in the overcast environment? It is a pleasure to report—what we all know, of course—that these attempts failed miserably. The enduring qualities of the old rhymes which had the rhythm and vigor to last through many centuries were too much for Mrs. Follen, though hers was truly an indomitable spirit.

Ann Taylor (1782-1866) and Jane Taylor (1783-1824). Two charming though moralistic poets who wrote verses for children were Ann and Jane Taylor. Born in London, they moved to Suffolk in the English countryside at an early age. Their happy home life in a pastoral surrounding of woods, birds, flowers, animals, and the open sky above is reflected in their verse. How else would one be on such friendly terms with the stars as was Jane Taylor?

> Twinkle, twinkle little star
> How I wonder where you are
> High above the clouds on high
> Like a diamond in the sky.[11]

The Taylors of Ongay were all engravers and publishers; mother, father, sisters, and brother, Isaac. The two girls, members of a literary and artistic family, began composing verses at an early age. The publishers, Darton and Harvey, wrote to Isaac Taylor requesting some easy verse for young children when "any of their harps were tuned and their muse in good humor." *Original Poems for Infant Minds* by Several Young Persons (1804) was published when Jane was twenty-one and Ann was twenty-two. Brother Isaac, age seventeen, also contributed a few verses to this collection. Some poems by Adelaide O'Keefe (1776-1855) were chosen by the publisher to fill out the volume.

The freshness and sparkle of the Taylors' verses won immediate favor with the reading public. In a sense, they wrote about people like themselves who led a pleasant and simple life. Soon the poems were translated into French, German, and Russian for continental consumption.

The verses often dealt with the commonplace events of childhood. For instance, kindness to animals is preached in Jane Taylor's "I Love Little Pussy."

---

[10]Monica Kiefer, *American Children through Their Books* (Philadelphia: University of Pennsylvania Press, 1948), pp. 22, 23.
[11]Jane Taylor, cited in May Hill Arbuthnot, *Arbuthnot Anthology of Children's Literature*, rev. ed. (Glenview, Ill.: Scott, Foresman & Co., 1961), p. 168.

I love little pussy,
    Her coat is so warm,
And if I don't hurt her,
    She'll do me no harm;
So I'll not pull her tail,
    Nor drive her away,
But Pussy and I
    Very gently will play.[12]

The Taylors often embodied ethical considerations in verse form:

My good little fellow, don't throw your ball there,
    You'll break the neighbor's windows, I know:
On the end of the house there is room, and to spare,
    Go round, you can have a delightful game there,
Without fearing for where you may throw.[13]

Though the penchant for moralizing so typical of the times removed the Taylors' poems from the realm of poetic artistry, their joy in life, their verve, and their fondness for children rings out clearly in the verses they wrote.

John Bunyan (1628-1688). The Puritan, John Bunyan, departed from this formula. In 1686, his *A Book for Boys and Girls or Country Rhymes for Children,* though steeped in allegorical comparisons, had a milder tone, and there were flashes of humor to be found.

But Hog, why look'st so big? Why dost so flounce,
So snort, and fling away? Dost thou renounce
Subjection to thy Lord cause he has fed thee?[14]

It was the only time he wrote specifically for young children, although his *Pilgrim's Progress* was preempted by them.

Isaac Watts (1674-1748). A nonconformist minister and writer of hymns, Isaac Watts, in 1715, gave to children some immortal "Divine and Moral Songs" which dwelt on the love and beneficence of God rather than on his wrath. Watts learned about children firsthand through tutoring the children of Sir John Hartop. He understood something about children's intellectual development—their capacities as well as their limitations at various stages of growth. Like John Bunyan, he perceived religion as a beautiful and majestic experience rather than as a harsh, unwavering, self-righteous, obeisance to a stern and judgmental God.

"Joy to the World" and "Oh God Our Help in Ages Past" are among the hymns which are sung by groups of people today with as much joy

---

[12]Jane Taylor, cited in Arbuthnot, *Anthology,* p. 48.
[13]Ann Taylor, cited in Arbuthnot, *Children and Books,* p. 139.
[14]Cornelia Meigs, et al. *Critical History,* p. 153.

as they were sung in 1715. Some of his verses were gentle and lulling as is the well-known and remembered "Cradle Song":

>Hush! my dear, lie still and slumber,
>Holy Angel's guard thy bed!
>Heavenly blessings without number
>Gently falling on thy head.[15]

His kindly gifts of verse have brought joy and comfort to succeeding generations of children and adults.

William Blake (1757-1827).   A true artist of poetic form was William Blake, whose poetry continues to have strong appeal for children. His verse is often hauntingly tender. Many of the poems have strong cadence and auditory appeal. His introduction to *Songs of Innocence,* "Piping Down the Valleys," explains how he came to write verses for children.

>Piping down the valleys wild,
>   Piping songs of pleasant glee,
>On a cloud I saw a child,
>   And he laughing said to me:
>
>"Pipe a song about a Lamb!"
>   So I piped with merry chear.
>"Piper, pipe that song again";
>   So I piped: he wept to hear.
>
>And I made a rural pen,
>   And I stain'd the water clear,
>And I wrote my happy songs
>   Every child may joy to hear.[16]

And he did. His *Songs of Innocence* was truly "piped" with a simplicity and freshness of expression. Though Blake may not have had children in mind as the target audience for his poetry as did Isaac Watts, his poems portray the innocence and wonder of youth before maturity sets in. They seem to meet children "where they live" and because of this, his verse has lived. Though Blake was unheralded in his own lifetime, his poems have lived on to attain recognition in the twentieth century.

Scholars have spent many years in painstaking research attempting to interpret and plumb the depths of the messages imbedded in Blake's poetry. For example, in "The Tiger," from *Songs of Experience,* universal questions of mankind, "Who am I?" and "Who made me?" are set to majestic music by William Blake.

---

[15]Isaac Watts, cited in Arbuthnot, *Children and Books,* p. 139.
[16]William Blake, cited in Walter Barnes, *The Children's Poets* (New York: World Book Co., 1925), p. 97.

Tyger! Tyger! burning bright
In the forests of the night,
What immortal hand or eye
Could frame thy fearful symmetry?

In what distant deeps or skies
Burnt the fire of thine eyes?
On what wings dare he aspire?
What the hand dare seize the fire?[17]

Imagination, artistry, and simplicity glow in the words with which Blake chose to speak to children. There is tenderness and understanding. The child's kinship with the poet in the eternal wondering and response to beauty and movement in life were sensitively expressed in the innocent songs of William Blake.

William Roscoe (1753-1831).

Come take up your hats and away let us haste
To the Butterfly's Ball and the Grasshopper feast—
The Trumpeter Gad-Fly has summoned the crew
And the revels are now only waiting for you.[18]

In this manner William Roscoe described a civic social function which he had attended, for the entertainment and amusement of his children. The verse was published in 1806 in the *Gentleman's Magazine* in London. The next year, Newbery's successor, John Harris, with his keen judgment of what would be popular and pleasing to children,

The Trumpeter, *Gad-Fly*, has summoned the crew. Reprinted by permission of Pantheon Books, a division of Random House, Inc., from *Flowers of Delight* by Leonard de Vries.

---

[17]Ibid., p. 95.
[18]Mrs. E. M. Field, *The Child and His Book*. 2d ed. (London: Wells, Gardner, Darton and Co., 1892), p. 289.

published the verse with fourteen hand-colored pictures. Twelve of these were the original pen and brush drawings of William Mulready.

Though Roscoe's poetry perhaps was not artistic according to certain criteria of this art form, its gaiety, rhythm, and obvious omission of any attempts to instruct or inform, plus the mischievous and good-humored drawings which gave human faces to the creatures, delighted adults and children alike.

"If the sincerest form of flattery be imitation, then certainly the author should have felt flattered."

Mrs. Dorset published *Peacock at Home* in the same year, 1807. It was reported that forty thousand copies of these two poems were sold in twelve months. The *British Critic* deplored the rash of imitations which followed, but this type of amusing verse about social functions and parties was apparently too tempting to pass up.

William Allingham (1824-1880). An Irish writer, William Allingham, took children on a flight with the fairies.

> Up the airy mountain,
> Down the rushy glen,
> We daren't go a-hunting
> For fear of little men;
> Wee folk, good folk,
> Trooping all together;
> Green jacket, red cap,
> And white owl's feather![19]

Born in Ballyshannon, Donegal, Ireland, he had the Irish gift of being able to see and talk with the "wee folk," and he recorded their songs and plights:

> An Elf sat on a twig,
> He was not very big,
> He sang a little song,
> He did not think it wrong;
> But he was on a Wizard's ground,
> Who hated all sweet sound.[20]

At middle age, William Allingham resigned a civil service post to become an editor of *Fraser's Magazine,* a well-known publication of the time. His *Rhymes for Young Folks,* published in 1887, was illustrated by Helen Allingham, Kate Greenaway, Caroline Peterson, and Harry Fainiss. This volume was republished by Macmillan in 1930 for their Little Library Series under the title *Robin Redbreast and Other Verses. The Fairy Shoemaker and Other Fairy Poems,* illustrated so

---

[19]William Allingham, cited in Miriam Blanton Huber, *Story and Verse for Children* (New York: Macmillan Co., 1965), p. 132.
[20]Ibid., p. 136.

accurately by Boris Artzybasheff, is another Allingham gift to children which the Macmillan company republished in 1928 for the continued enjoyment of young people.

William Brighty Rands (1823-1882). What a "Great, wide, beautiful, wonderful World" it was to William Brighty Rands who personified it in verse so that future generations might also marvel at its beauty and vastness.

> Great, wide, beautiful, wonderful World,
> With the wonderful water round you curled,
> And the wonderful grass upon your breast,
> World, you are beautifully dressed.[21]

Writing under the pseudonyms of Henry Holbeach and Matthew Browne, he published *Lilliput Levee* in 1867, *Lilliput Lectures* in 1871 (primarily prose selections), and *Lilliput Lyrics* in 1899. The latter volume was edited by R. Bromley Johnson and illustrated by Charles Robinson. In addition to many new poems, it also contained verses from his first two books as well as ones that had been published in magazines. Best loved by children of bygone years and children of today is Rand's poem about the inimitable nondoor-shutter with the funny and alliterative name.

> Godfrey Gordon Gustavus Gore.
> No doubt you have heard the name before—
> Was a boy who never would shut a door!
>
> The wind might whistle, the wind might roar,
> And teeth be aching and throats be sore,
> But still he never would shut the door.
>
> His father would beg, his mother implore,
> "Godfrey Gordon Gustavus Gore,
> We really do wish you would shut the door!"
>
> Their hands they wrung, their hair they tore;
> But Godfrey Gordon Gustavus Gore
> Was deaf as the buoy out at the Nore.[22]

Christina Rossetti (1830-1894). As her collection of verse, *Sing Song,* published in 1872, attests, Christina Rossetti truly did sing songs for children. She was *en rapport* with children's interest and ability to attend to and appreciate the life around them, from little bugs—

> Brown and furry
> Caterpillar in a hurry;
> Take your walk
> To the shady leaf or stalk.[23]

---

[21]William Brighty Rands, cited in Arbuthnot, *Anthology,* pp. 207-208.
[22]Ibid., p. 129.
[23]Christina Rossetti, cited in Huber, *Story and Verse,* p. 105.

to larger mice—

> The city mouse lives in a house;
> The garden mouse lives in a bower,
> He's friendly with the frogs and toads,
> And sees the pretty plants and flower,
>
> The city mouse eats bread and cheese;
> The garden mouse eats what he can;
> We will not grudge him seeds and stalks,
> Poor little timid furry man.[24]

and even to arching rainbows—

> There are bridges on the rivers,
> As pretty as you please;
> But the bow that bridges heaven,
> And overtops the trees
> And builds a road from earth to sky,
> Is prettier far than these.[25]

A delicate child of highly intellectual and artistic parents, Christina was an invalid during much of her life. Her poems for children provided a somewhat imperceptible transition from the pedantic or nonsense verses of her time to the artistic cadences of truly poetic utterances.

Fun, Nonsense, and Humor

Edward Lear (1812-1888).

> There was an Old Man with a beard,
> Who said: "It is just as I feared!—
> Two Owls and a Hen,
> Four Larks and a Wren,
> Have all built their nest in my beard!"[26]

Morals? Lessons? Manners? Indeed not. Rhymes, rhythm, and meter in words both real and invented which nudge funny bones into delicious laughter.

Lear is the first poet who set out deliberately to conjure up gaiety, fun, and laughter in his verses. One of twenty-one surviving children of a wealthy family, he had two misfortunes in life which might have stifled the humor of a less buoyant spirit. His "Terrible Demon" with which he lived throughout life was a mild form of epilepsy. The loss of financial security was also a shocking experience to a sickly child. When Edward was only thirteen, his father was thrown into a debtor's prison, and his mother was left to cope with poverty.

---

[24]Ibid., p. 106.
[25]Ibid., p. 115.
[26]Edward Lear, cited in Arbuthnot, *Children and Books*, p. 121.

Of Lear's talents, that of graphic art was the first to flower. He was commissioned to visit the Earl of Derby's estate to make drawings of the birds and animals. It was in this country atmosphere that the irrepressible nonsense verse bubbled up and took form as the first *Book of Nonsense,* published in 1846. *More Nonsense* followed in 1872. *Nonsense Songs, Stories, Botany and Alphabets* was published in 1871. *Laughable Lyrics,* which contained "The Dong with the Luminous Nose," "The Pelican Chorus," and the "Quangle-Wangle's Hat," among others, appeared in 1877. These volumes, accompanied by Lear's masterfully executed, hilariously imaginative and seemingly naive drawings are a legacy of fun and laughter—a literary heritage to be cherished and enjoyed by adults and children for all time. How fortunate we are that Edward Lear did not "giggle heartily and hop on one leg down the great gallery" as he became bored with the "uniform apathetic tone assumed by lofty society."[27] The world must be forever grateful that he took refuge instead with the Earl's innumerable grandchildern for whom he created wonderful and immortal nonsense as

The Jumblies

They went to sea in a sieve, they did;
   In a sieve they went to sea;
In spite of all their friends could say,
On a winter's morn, on a stormy day,
   In a sieve they went to sea.
And when the sieve turned round and round,
And every one cried, "You'll all be drowned!"
They called aloud, "Our sieve ain't big;
But we don't care a button, we don't care a fig:
   In a sieve we'll go to sea!"
     Far and few, far and few,
      Are the lands where the Jumblies live:
      Their heads are green, and their hands are blue;
      And they went to sea in a sieve.[28]

Laura E. Richards (1850-1943). Tirra Lirra, the title of Laura E. Richards' collection of poems, suggests the rhythm of her verse. She was the daughter of talented parents. Her father was Samuel Gridley Howe, philanthropist, author, and teacher of the blind, and her mother was Julia Ward Howe, singer of note and composer of "The Battle Hymn of the Republic." Singing was an integral part of the Howe family life.

As her own seven children were growing, Laura Richards made up verses to lull and amuse them. Spontaneous and fresh as the morn, the lyrical quality of her verse literally makes the words sing.

---

[27]Ibid., p. 118.
[28]Edward Lear, cited in Arbuthnot, *Anthology,* pp. 134-5.

Young children respond wholeheartedly to Laura E. Richards' gay nonsense and to her funny inventiveness with words which roll around on the tongue and portray such hilarious and confusing situations as the poor elephant who tried to use the "telephant." And there were those two amusing ladies, "Mrs. Snipkin and Mrs. Wobblechin."

Mrs. Richards' verses were first published in *St. Nicholas,* a neophyte magazine, in 1873, at the suggestion of her husband. Her first collection of verses, *In My Nursery,* was published in 1890. In 1932, Mary Lamberton Becker combined the poems that appeared in this first book with other Richards verses, culminating in the delightful *Tirra Lirra.* A poet of the nursery, child life, gaiety, and nonsense, Laura Richards combined a mother's insight with facile talent. Her artistry in spinning out delightful tunes on her "hurdy-gurdy" remained undiminished even at fourscore plus years of age when her great-grandchildren made up her audience.

Walter de la Mare (1873-1956). The quality of Walter de la Mare's poems for children, the beauty, grace, poetic word pictures, and wonderfully lyrical style have earned him the critics' accolade as the greatest of modern poets for children.

SILVER

> Slowly, silently, now the moon
> Walks the night in her silver shoon;
> This way, and that, she peers, and sees
> Silver fruit upon silver trees;
> One by one the casements catch
> Her beams beneath the silvery thatch;
> Couched in his kennel, like a log,
> With paws of silver, sleeps the dog;
> From their shadowy cote the white breasts peep
> Of doves in a silver-feathered sleep;
> A harvest mouse goes scampering by,
> With silver claws, and silver eye;
> And moveless fish in the water gleam,
> By silver reeds in a silver stream.[29]

In his children's anthology, *Tom Tiddler's Ground,* de la Mare talks with children about some of the poems. He comments on Shelley's "The Question" in this manner:

The *sounds* of the words of poetry resemble the sounds of music. They are a pleasure and delight merely to listen to, as they rise and fall and flow and pause and echo—like the singing of birds at daybreak or a little before the fall of night when the daffodils "take the winds of March with beauty." It is a great pleasure also to *say* the words aloud—as well and clearly and carefully as one possibly can:

---

[29]Walter de la Mare, cited in Arbuthnot, *Anthology,* p. 118. Reprinted by permission of the Literary Trustees of Walter de la Mare and The Society of Authors as their representative.

"Green cowbind and the moonlight coloured may," or "flowers azure black and streaked with gold." Try it.[30]

Walter de la Mare continues to knock at many "wee small doors" as he captivates the imagination of the wee small children and larger children the world over.

> Some one came knocking
>   At my wee, small door;
> Some one came knocking,
>   I'm sure—sure—sure;
> I listened, I opened,
>   I looked to left and right,
> But nought there was a-stirring
>   In the still dark night.[31]

Robert Louis Stevenson (1850-1894). Robert Louis Stevenson wrote in verse of the happenings both real and fanciful which he remembered fondly from his own childhood. Many of these experiences in turn touched chords of remembrance in adults, and they appealed to children because the words in which they were so tunefully told described the things they did. For instance,

> How do you like to go up in a swing,
> Up in the air so blue?
> Oh, I do think it the pleasantest thing
> Ever a child can do![32]

What child hasn't been fascinated with his inescapable shadow which shortens, lengthens, and darts and dips in unison with himself?

> I have a little shadow that goes in and out with me,
> And what can be the use of him is more than I can see.
> He is very, very like me from the heels up to the head;
> And I see him jump before me, when I jump into my bed.[33]

A Child's Garden of Verses was first published in 1885 as *Penny Whistles.* It contained sixty-three poems and was dedicated to Stevenson's childhood nurse, Alison Cunningham. Some of these poems simply tell about children—a reminiscence of childhood—but many are part and parcel of the child himself.

Treasure Island, a landmark in novels for children, will be discussed in Chapter 6; but one who often was called "the poet laureate of childhood" must have his place here among the poets, too.

A. A. Milne (1882-1956). A modern writer who must be recorded in both poetry and prose accounts, too, is A. A. Milne. The verses con-

---

[30]Walter de la Mare, cited in Lillian Smith, *The Unreluctant Years* (Chicago: American Library Association, 1953), p. 100.

[31]Cited in Huber, *Story and Verse for Children,* p. 132. Reprinted by permission of Holt, Rinehart & Winston.

[32]Robert Louis Stevenson, *A Child's Garden of Verses,* in Huber, p. 89.

[33]Ibid., p. 90.

tained in *When We Were Very Young,* published in 1924, and in *Now We Are Six,* published in 1927, have universal appeal. For example:

> Once upon a time there were three little foxes,
> Who didn't wear stockings and they didn't wear sockses.
> But they all had handkerchiefs to blow their noses,
> And they kept their handkerchiefs in cardboard boxes.[34]

> If I were a bear
>   And a big bear, too,
> I shouldn't much care
>   If it froze or snew;
> I shouldn't much mind if it snowed or friz—
> I'd be all fur-lined with a coat like his![35]

Many other singers of songs for children should be recorded because of their marvelous penchant for looking at the world in a vivid, intense manner as children do. They have communicated their observations in rhythmic pictures which have enabled children to see, smell, taste, hear, or move with this phenomenon. Carl Sandburg's *Chicago Poems*; Eleanor Farjeon's Christmas poems in *Come Christmas*; Rose Fyleman's fairy poems in *Fairies and Chimneys*; and Robert Frost's *You Come Too: Favorite Poems for Young Readers,* published in 1959 when he was eighty-five years old, are just a few of the many notable contributions to the child's world of song, melody, laughter, gaiety, wonder, and beauty—a part of their literary heritage, their life, and their world.

QUESTIONS AND SUGGESTIONS

1. Choose and review several editions of Mother Goose. Compare their content, format, and illustrations. What do you believe to be the basic appeals for young children in these nursery rhymes?
2. Compare the verses of Ann and Jane Taylor with those of Laura E. Richards. Are there any similar qualities? What are the striking differences?
3. Read a representative number of Walter de la Mare's poems. Choose a contemporary children's poet of merit and do the same. Try to identify common qualities which make this poetry distinctive.
4. Read a representative sampling from the works of the early poets for children cited in the chapter. What seems to have been the qualities in poetry which appealed to children of yesterday? Are these qualities enduring? Try some of these poems with children.

---

[34]From *Now We Are Six,* by A. A. Milne, p. 142. Copyright 1927, by E. P. Dutton & Co., Inc. Renewal, 1955, by A. A. Milne. Used by permission of the publishers.
[35]Ibid., p. 89. Reprinted by permission of E. P. Dutton & Co.

SELECTED CHAPTER REFERENCES

ADAMS, BESS PORTER. *About Books and Children.* New York: Holt, Rinehart & Winston, 1953.

ARBUTHNOT, MAY HILL. *Anthology of Children's Literature,* rev. ed. Glenview, Ill.: Scott, Foresman & Co., 1961.

———. *Children and Books,* Glenview, Ill.: Scott, Foresman & Co., 1964.

BARNES, WALTER. *The Children's Poets.* New York: World Book Co., 1925.

DE VRIES, LEONARD. *Flowers of Delight:* An Agreeable Garland of Prose and Poetry. New York: Pantheon Books, 1966.

FIELD, MRS. E. M. *The Child and His Book.* 2d ed. London: Wells, Gardner, Darton and Co., 1892.

HUBER, MIRIAM BLANTON. *Story and Verse for Children.* New York: Macmillan Co., 1965.

KIEFER, MONICA. *American Children through Their Books.* Philadelphia: University of Pennsylvania Press, 1948.

MEIGS, CORNELIA; EATON, ANNE; NESBITT, ELIZABETH; and VIGUERS, RUTH HILL. *A Critical History of Children's Literature.* New York: Macmillan Co., 1953.

MUIR, PERCY. *English Children's Books: 1600-1900* New York: Frederick A. Praeger, Publishers, 1954.

OPIE, IONA and PETER, eds. *The Oxford Dictionary of Nursery Rhymes.* Oxford: The Clarendon Press, 1951.

SMITH, LILLIAN. *The Unreluctant Years.* Chicago: American Library Association, 1953.

THOMAS, KATHERINE, ELWES. *The Real Personages of Mother Goose.* New York: William Morrow & Co., 1930.

WATTS, ISAAC. *Divine and Moral Song.* London: James Nisbet and Co., 1866.

chapter 5

realism — remember thy creator, thy lessons, and thy manners

During the fourteenth and fifteenth centuries, children of farmers became farmers and toiled in the fields throughout their lives. The children of tradesmen were usually apprenticed at the age of seven or eight and learned a trade. It was the custom for children of the upper classes to become wards of members of royal families or to serve the nobility as pages, maids, and so forth.

There were a few grammar schools for children of the upper classes; the apprenticed children sometimes received a minimal education from their masters; and some of them, plus a few children of the poor, were fortunate enough to be able to attend the monastery schools. But there were far too few of these schools, and so only a small proportion of the young population received any education.

During the fifteenth and sixteenth centuries, the growth of the towns and the guilds, with the concomitant development of a middle-class society, resulted in a great increase in grammar schools.

This steadily increasing momentum in both hope and desire for education stimulated the publishing of lesson books for children. Adams classified these under three divisions: "(1) manners, social and domestic arts; (2) elementary English and religious education; (3) general school-books, often intended for adults as well as children."[1]

Lesson Books

The Horn Book. In the days before printing, children had few lesson books which they might hold while they studied from them. They had wax tablets, slates, or other writing materials on which to write, but the hornbook was one of the earliest printed lesson books for children which they themselves might handle. These little books—which

---

[1]Bess Porter Adams, *About Books and Children* (New York: Holt, Rinehart & Winston, 1953), p. 20.

were really not books at all—were two and three-quarter by five inch pieces of wood cut in the shape of a paddle on which were pasted lesson sheets protected by a piece of transparent horn fastened to the wood with narrow brass strips called "lattens."

The lesson sheet was made of vellum or parchment in earlier horn-books, and later of paper. The ✛ (Christ's cross) was placed at the beginning of the first line, and followed by as much of the alphabet as space permitted. The alphabet in lower case was followed by the capital letters, then the single vowels and the vowel combinations, and sometimes the nine digits. The Lord's Prayer filled the rest of the space.

Some hornbooks ended the Lord's Prayer according to the Roman Church's "deliver us from all evil." During the reigns of Queen Elizabeth and the two Stuarts, the cross was omitted, and the prayer ended with "for Thine is the kingdom, the power and glory, forever and ever, So be it."[2]

For centuries, the little hornbook was used to teach children their letters. There were many variations in the hornbooks, as may be noted in a study of them in the various private collections, libraries, and museums. There were even gingerbread hornbooks for some of our ancestors to enjoy after they had studied their lessons well.

In these collections may be found hornbooks hand-printed in manu-script, hornbooks printed in the black-letter type used in early printing or in the elegant Roman type which was developed and used widely in the sixteenth century. The materials differed, too. They were made of wood, ivory, leather, and various metals, although wood backs were the most common. Some hornbooks had an abacus attached to the back. The Queen Elizabeth hornbook is an example of the elegance of some of these little books. Its backing is of equisitely filigreed silver over red silk.

Whether made of silver, wood, or gingerbread, the hornbook was the vehicle for learning the alphabet until developments in paper-making and engraving brought other lesson books.

The Battledore. A successor to the hornbook (about 1770) was a lesson book called the battledore (so named because of its shape), which was made of stiff paper folded so as to make two leaves and a flap. The earliest of these was covered with gilt-embossed Dutch paper. The lesson side was varnished. There was room for more easy reading lessons and little woodcuts in addition to the alphabet and the Lord's Prayer. Sometimes a short fable or a didactic story was included. These thrice-folded lesson books were stiff enough to use as battledores when not in use as schoolbooks.

---

[2]Beulah Folmsbee, *A Little History of the Horn Book* (Boston: The Horn Book, 1942), pp. 1-31.

Battledores must have been extremely popular lesson books. What could be handier than this double use of a schoolbook? However, some books were not as entertaining.

The New-England Primer. According to Puritan theology, no priest, masses, or prayers were to be used in religious pursuits. Each person had a moral responsibility to seek and find his own salvation. But it was important that individuals know how to read so that they might use the Bible to show them the way. This was the Puritan philosophy of education. Children of very tender years were taught and drilled upon the tenets which they were to "think out for themselves when they reached the age of discretion." *The New-England Primer* became the vehicle for the teaching of reading for more than 150 years. It thus became a tool for religious indoctrination.

The method of combining the alphabet for the purpose of teaching the child to read and the catechism to teach religious precepts in the same book was employed since the beginning of printing. *The Enschedé Abecedarium,* printed in the fifteenth century, contained the alphabet, the Pater Noster, the Ave Maria, the Credo, and two other prayers. "The Book of Hours," translated from Latin to English as the "Prymer of Salisbury use," was printed as early as 1490.[3]

Many unauthorized primers were printed in the time of Henry VIII. At first, he issued proclamations against them, but in 1534 when he separated from the church of Rome, he authorized the issuance of the *Reform Primer.* Less than a year later, he licensed the issue of a *Goodly Prymer in Englysshe.*

A third time, a new and only path to heaven was charted by Henry VIII in a primer known as the *Henry VIII Primer.* All of the primers contained instructions for children. The ABC Book, a preliminary part of all the primers of the times, "contained the alphabet, the Lord's Prayer, the Hail Mary, the Creed, various Graces for before and after 'dyner' and for 'fysshe dayes,' and the 'ten commaundements'."[4]

The issuance by the king of so many primers each professing to contain the precepts of the true faith, that is "The Primer set forth by the King's Majesty, and his clergy to be taught, learned and read and none other be used throughout all his dominions, 1545. *Cum privilegio ad imprimendum solum,*"[5] became confusing and unsettling to the people. Some groups developed beliefs and rituals of their own and refused to buy the primer which changed with each whim of the king. Other primers were being printed. Who was to determine which contained the true prayers and catechism?

---

[3]Paul Leicester Ford, *The New-England Primer* (New York: Teachers College, Columbia University, 1962), p. 4.
[4]Ibid., p. 5.
[5]Ibid., p. 5.

All these primers were not intended as schoolbooks. They were "primary" manuals of church service and forerunners to the "Book of Common Prayer." This is how they attained the name of "primer."

ABC books had previously been printed cheaply and sold for a small sum whereas the primers were expensive. Publishers who belonged to separatist groups saw the possibilities of combining the primer and the ABC book into one book.

The earliest known combination of the schoolbook-catechism was Bastingius' *Catechisme of Christiane Religion, taught in scholes,* printed in Edinburgh in 1591. The ABC was prefixed to it. Bishop Bedell's catechism, printed in Dublin in 1631, is another early example of this style.[6]

In 1686, Benjamin Harris fled London for the colonies and set up a printing establishment in Boston. He was an ardent Protestant and had been in trouble with the authorities in England for his printing of *A Protestant Petition,* the *Protestant Tutor,* and other religious tracts. The *Protestant Tutor* was designed to develop in children an aversion to popery. In Boston, Harris abridged the *"Tutor"* and renamed it the *New-England Primer.* It is believed that the first edition was issued between 1687 and 1690. It met with immediate success. There is no extant copy of this first edition. Upon his return to England, Harris published the Primer, changing the title to *The New English Tutor.* But it was in New England that it achieved its greatest success. For over one hundred years, it was *the* schoolbook of the dissenters in America, and it was frequently reprinted during the next hundred years. It is estimated that, during this period, it probably reached total sales of three million copies.

Throughout its various printings over the years it was in use, printers made changes to suit their tastes or business interests. There are certain identifying features, however, which earmark every edition of the *New-England Primer.*

They all began with the letters of the alphabet, followed by various pages which contained vowels, consonants, double letters, italics, and capitals. These were followed by "Easy Syllables for Children" (the syllabarium), *ab, eb, ib, ob, ub,* which in turn were followed by words of one syllable, lengthening by degrees to words of six syllables. When the printer lacked space he often dropped out the polysyllabic words. This progression of alphabet and syllables is identical in the hornbooks used in this period, too.

One salient feature of the ABC books which is omitted in the *New-England Primer* is the cross at the beginning of the alphabet. It had invariably been placed there in other primers and hornbooks. Because

---

[6]Ibid., pp. 8-9.

of this, the first line was called "Christ's Cross Row," and eventually was shortened to "Chris, Cross Row."

An alphabet of *Lessons for Youth* followed. These were sentences from the Bible arranged so that each began with a successive capital letter of the alphabet, for example, for "G"— "Grieve not the Holy Spirit," and for "S"—"Salvation belongeth to the Lord." No word could be found for "X," and so we find "Xhort one another daily while is (is) called to day, lest any of you be hardened through the deceitfulness of Sin."[7]

TRuſt in God at all times ye peopl‚
pour out your hearts before him.
UPon the wicked God ſhall rain an
horrible 'Tempeſt.
WO to the wicked, it ſhall be iⅡ
with him, for the reward of his
hands ſhall be given him.
EXHort one another daily while is
is called to day, leſt any of you
be hardened through the deceitfulneſs of
Sin.
YOung Men ye have overcome the
wicked one.
ZEal hath confumed me, becauſe thy
enemies have forgotten the words
of God.   *Choice Sentences.*
1. Praying will make thee leave ſin
ning, or ſinning will make thee leave
praying.
2. Our Weakneſs and Inabilities break
not the bond of our Duties.
3. What we are afraid to ſpeak before
Men, we ſhould be afraid to think before
God.
              The

A page from the Alphabet of Lessons from the *New-England Primer* by Paul Leicester Ford.

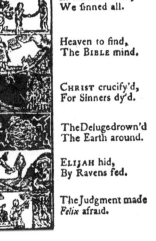

A	In ADAM's Fall, We finned all.
B	Heaven to find, The BIBLE mind.
C	CHRIST crucify'd, For Sinners dy'd.
D	TheDelugedrown'd The Earth around.
E	ELIJAH hid, By Ravens fed.
F	TheJudgment made *Felix* afraid.

Rhymed Alphabet Pages

(From the "New England Primer." Boſton : 1762)

First page of alphabetical rhymes and pictures from the *New-England Primer* by Paul Leicester Ford.

Printed by permission of Teachers College Press, Columbia University, New York.

The Lord's Prayer and the Apostle's Creed usually followed the "Alphabet of Lessons." Then came twenty-four little pictures with alpha-betical rhymes starting with the famous

In Adam's Fall,
We sinned all.

After the rhymed alphabet is the picture of John Rogers burning at the stake, "His Wife, with nine small children, and one at her Breast, following him to the Stake, with which sorrowful sight he was not in the least daunted, but with wonderful Patience died courageously for the Gospel of Jesus Christ.

---

[7]Ibid., page unnumbered.

"Some few Days before his Death, he writ the following Exhortation to his Children.

> Give ear my Children to my words,
>   whom God hath dearly bought,
> Lay up his Laws within your heart,
>   and print them in your thought.
> I leave you here a little Book,
>   for you to look upon;
> That you may see your Fathers face,
>   when he is dead and gone.
> Who for the hope of heavenly things,
>   while he did here remain,
> Gave over all his golden Years,
>   to Prison and to Pain.
>
> Commit no Sin in any wise,
>   keep his Commandement.
> Abhor that arrant Whore of Rome,
>   and all her Blasphemies;
> And drink not of her cursed Cup,
>   obey not her decrees."[8]

Following John Rogers' dismal, doleful address to his children is "The Shorter Catechism," the familiar question-and-answer format. In all eighteenth century catechisms examined by Ford,[9] he found either the Westminister Assembly's *Shorter Catechism* or John Cotton's *Spiritural Milk for Babes.* In some editions, both were included.

Spiritual Milk for Boston Babes: Drawn out of the breasts of both Testaments for their Souls' nourishment, But may be of like use to any children, was compiled by John Cotton and is believed to have been printed at Cambridge by Doye between 1641 and 1645. This approved catechism was the first book for children printed in America. It read as follows:

Q. What hath God done for you?
A. God hath made me, he keepeth me, and he can save me.
Q. What is God?
A. God is a Spirit of himself and for himself.
Q. How many Gods be there?
A. There be but One GOD in three Persons, the Father, the Son, and the Holy Ghost.
Q. How did God make you?
A. In my first parents holy and righteous.
Q. Are you then born holy and righteous?
A. No, my first parents sinned, and I in them.
Q. Are you then a sinner?
A. I was conceived in Sin and born in Iniquity.

---

[8]Ibid., pages unnumbered.
[9]Ibid., pages unnumbered.

Q. What is your birth sin?
A. Adam's Sin imputed to me and a corrupt Nature dwelling in me.[10]

At first, John Cotton's *Spiritual Milk for Boston Babes* retained its popularity, but the *New-England Primer* steadily gained favor and finally outdistanced the former in sales and staying power for many long years.

Information Books. Volumes treating secular subjects with the intent of disseminating information were appearing with greater frequency by the second half of the seventeenth century.

Henry Winstanly's *All the Principal Nations of the World Presented in their Habits of Fashions of Dressing* was a 1665 forerunner of modern travel books. Though the geographical content was less than authentic, California being identified as a South Sea island, the attempt at broadening children's earthly horizons as opposed to concentrating only on the heavenly horizon was commendable.

The eighteenth century saw more attempts at disseminating information in books for children. Isaac Watts, in 1726, wrote *The Knowledge of the Heavens and the Earth Made Easy*, or *The First Principles of Geography and Astronomy Explained*; Tommy Trip's *History of Birds and Beasts*, in 1771; and *The Circle of the Sciences*, 1745, were two of the Newbery information books later pirated and reprinted by Isaiah Thomas in America.[11]

Textbooks other than the Primers were slow in finding their way into the schools. Noah Webster's *Blue Backed Speller, Simplified and Standardized American Spelling*, published in 1783, was a standard in America for many years. In 1801, Sir Richard Phillips published William Mavor's *English Spelling Book* which remained persistently successful in England.

Geographies, arithmetic books, and science books followed. The publication of these textbooks was stimulated by the increase in the number of schools which, in turn, was due to a growing middle-class population, the result of expanding commerce and trade.

Remember Thy Manners

John E. Mason's *Gentlefolk in the Making* is a study of the courtesy literature printed during the period between 1531 and 1774. Four kinds of courtesy literature are distinguished in this work: polite conduct, policy, civility, and parental advice.

---

[10]Cited in Adams, *About Books and Children*, p. 78.
[11]Charlotte S. Huck and Doris Young Kuhn, *Children's Literature in the Elementary School*. 2d ed. (New York: Holt, Rinehart & Winston, 1968), pp. 64-65.

These books of advice were very similar in nature. Most of the writers covered substantially the same topics. Children were counseled on "gentlemanly and ungentlemanly pursuits, housekeeping, the choice of companions and friends and wife, and the care of children and servants."[12]

The courtesy books seemed to have originated in France and Italy and were imitated or copied in England. Among these early books was *Fifty Courtesies for the Table,* compiled by Fra Bonvicino in 1290. Another early book in manuscript, dating from about 1430-1440, is the *Boke of Courtesye.* Its 848 rhymed lines exhort the young man "not to fight at the table, make faces at his neighbor, stuff his mouth too full, eat noisily, spit on the table, or claw the dog."[13]

Caxton's *Book of Courtesye* was printed in 1497, and *The Book of Nurture* was written by Hugh Rhodes in 1530. These were the forerunners of an outpouring of courtesy and manners books in penny chapbook form throughout the seventeenth century and well into the eighteenth century. Examples of these are *The Parents Pious Gift* (1704) and *The Aged Fathers' Blessing* (1708). In the nineteenth century, Henry Ward Beecher, Hugh Blair, and many others wrote with didactic tones. "The urge of man to pour out prudent morality and pass on his wisdom to his children continues in twentieth century writing."[14]

Remember Thy Creator

During Queen Elizabeth's reign and well into the nineteenth century, most books for children were printed for the purposes of teaching religion, manners, and morals. Due to the Puritan influence in England and America, the fanciful, romantic stories which children previously had been reading in chapbook form were considered frivolous and harmful diversions from the true purpose of living the holy, godly life. Any digressions from the righteous path, it was believed, would lead to perdition. To the Puritans, life was real and life was earnest. Play, fun, amusement, and entertainment must be put aside. The child was considered to be "a miserable little sinner, full of original sin, and surrounded by snares and pitfalls from which escape was desperately difficult."[15] Guardian Angels who had been busy protecting their cherubic human counterparts before the Reformation were now superseded by the devil.

---

[12]William Sloane, *Children's Books in England and America in the Seventeenth Century* (New York: King's Crown Press, Columbia University Press, 1955), p. 33.
[13]Adams, *About Books and Children,* p. 22.
[14]Sloane, *Children's Books,* p. 42-43.
[15]Mrs. E. M. Field, *The Child and His Book,* 2d ed., (London: Wells, Gardner, Darton and Co., 1892), p. 188.

Sternness and harshness were the manifestations of parental love. The child must not be spared the rod, his spirit must be broken, and physical beauty, grace, and charm were suspect. Any of these attributes might be put to the devil's use.

The Puritans considered John Foxe's *Book of Martyrs* excellent reading for children since it exemplified the extent to which these holy individuals remained staunch and firm in their religious beliefs. Though this book was published in 1563, it attained its greatest popularity during the period of the Puritan and other separatist movements.

A zealous Protestant, Foxe was expelled from Magdalen College. While exiled in Germany and Switzerland for awhile during Queen Mary's reign, he began the book as an expression of the distress and resistance he felt to the idea that men and women could be put to death because of religious beliefs. He championed the causes of people who had been imprisoned as nonconformists, writing letters in their behalf and visiting them in their cells. Despite all his efforts, the inhumane slaughter persisted.

He became obsessed with the idea of documenting the history of martyrdom from the early beginnings in Rome when Christians were tossed to wild beasts, through the period of the Spanish Inquisitions and St. Bartholomew's massacre, to his own time when religious executions were taking place under both Elizabeth and Mary. He listened to stories of eyewitnesses and consulted all available records. Latimer's, Ridley's, and John Rogers' martyrdom, among others, were faithfully recorded. Each is a brief, separate biography which tells of heroism and a violent death.[16]

The *Book of Martyrs* is a historical record of man's intolerance of his fellowman and of inhumanity among men. The uses to which the Puritans put this work were really diametrically opposed to Foxe's purpose in writing it. The Puritans used it as a torch to keep religious intolerance alive, whereas it was written as a commentary on the incredible savagery and brutality in man which can make him capable of such prejudice. For children, the *Book of Martyrs* was frightening and horrifying.

James Janeway, as opposed to Foxe, wrote infamous books addressed to children for the purpose of indoctrinating them with a fanatic religious obsession. These were *Looking Glass for Children* and *Token for Children: being an Exact Account of the Conversion, Holy and Exemplary Lives and Joyful Deaths of Several Young Children*. In the latter books, toys are forbidden, and abstinence from all forms of relaxation and enjoyment is rewarded. Children are exhorted to rejoice at funerals of the blessed, to guard against the wiles of Satan, and so forth.

---

[16]Cornelia Meigs et al., *A Critical History of Children's Literature* (New York: Macmillan Co., 1953), pp. 42-44.

The poor misguided Puritans! They wanted their children to be happy for eternity but imbued their earthly lives with tales of morbid and frightening experiences.

The Bible becomes entertaining and recreational reading when compared to the sagas mentioned above, and it was considered just that by the Puritans. It was the Book without which there would be no guide in the path to salvation. But it was the one true storybook which the children had.

The Female Admonishers Plus Male Moralizers

The disequilibrium in religious, political, and philosophical thought resulting from the American Revolution, and then followed by the French Revolution, the influence of Locke's philosophy, and the confusion arising from Church fragmentation—Protestant groups, Papism, and the Church of England—were forces which propelled adults to cling to the old mores in an effort to keep the wobbling ship of state steady. The manner in which they sought to do this was by preaching and teaching to youth the morals and manners which they themselves held dear.

Until this period, religion had been the primary concern in the education of the child. Reaction to Puritanism was in the making. However, the reaction could not go far because the opposite extreme was Papism which, to most Englishmen and colonials of that day, was abhorrent. And so, in an attempt to chart a course between these two extremes, they tried to maintain their own version of a commendatory and highly respectable morality. The emphasis now in the education of children was not "Be good and you will go to heaven," nor "Be good, or else you will go to hell."[17] Instead, the stress was on manners and morals. Behavioral admonishments for every aspect of daily living were the themes in books for children. In these stories, those who did not heed the admonishments fell into the most dreadful state.

> The most trivial incident may point its trivial moral, and help to guide youth in the paths of Virtue (capital V). Does the untidy boy forget to tie his shoe? Straightway he will fall downstairs, and papa, before proceeding to call in nurse or doctor, will administer the appropriate lecture. "See, my child, the consequences of a bad habit," &c. The children are always represented as perfectly free agents, choosing the evil or the good, and being rewarded or punished in consequence, papa and mamma administering praise and reward, or reproof and correction, but the child's own happiness or misery being entirely its own affair. Thus, for instance, it was no fault of mamma's if "little Jack" "ran to play
> > Too far from home a long, long way,
> > And did not ask mamma."

[17]Field, *Child and His Book,* pp. 247, 248.

Nemesis promptly and properly overtakes Jack—
"So he was lost, and now must creep
Up chimney crying Sweep, Sweep, Sweep."[18]

Percy Muir uses the appellation "A Monstrous Regiment" to designate the group of women and a few men who took it upon themselves to write for young people in the latter half of the eighteenth century. Up until this time, books for children, for the most part, either had been written or compiled by the publisher, commissioned from hack writers, or had been produced as an extracurricular venture. As it became evident that juvenile books were a marketable commodity, a number of women authors emerged.[19]

Sarah Fielding (1710-1768). In 1749, Sarah Fielding, the sister of Henry Fielding, the novelist, published her only book for children. It was entitled *The Governess or The Little Female Academy.* The story line had to do with the establishment of a school for girls, a place that offered an environment in which might blossom and flourish the finest and most exemplary of young women.

Mrs. Teachem, the head of the institution, was a woman who was extremely democratic (but also extremely smug!). The girls were permitted to learn from one another what was proper during their "girlish" chats in the summerhouse. The names of the girls indicated the general direction of the learning—Miss Jenny Peace, Miss Lucy Sly, and so forth.

Though the dull behavioral narratives were interspersed with some romantic fanciful tales including giants and fairies, Mrs. Teachem tolled "the death knell to the fairies" by warning that such supernatural phenomena in a story was implanted only to divert and amuse and therefore must be read with sane and sober realization of this purpose.

Mrs. Trimmer brought out a revised edition of *The Governess* in 1820, omitting altogether the undesirable material of the first printing, that is, the fairy tales!

Mrs. Barbauld (1743-1825). During the latter part of the eighteenth century, Anna Laetitia (Aiken) Barbauld became a prominent figure in London literary society. Though her publications for children were only a small portion of her efforts, her impact was great. Her first book of poems, and later some of her books of prose, were written in collaboration with her brother, John. Later, she and her husband, the Reverend Rochemont Barbauld, established a boarding school for boys at Palgrave, Suffolk. She enjoyed teaching these students, adopting a conversational—almost Socratic—method, a method which she also used in writing.

---

[18]Ibid., p. 248.
[19]Percy Muir, *English Children's Books: 1600-1900* (New York: Frederick A. Praeger, Publishers, 1954), p. 82.

Mrs. Barbauld was an indefatigable teacher. No opportunity was too insignificant. She found a lesson to be taught in every moment and in every facet of living. As if this were not enough damage to wreak, she did her small and sincere bit to banish fairies and to try to breathe life into the fading allegorical style in prose writing.

Dorothy and Mary Jane Kilner. The pseudonym, "M. P.", was used by Dorothy Kilner, and "S. S." was used by her sister, Mary Jane. Though considerable uncertainty surrounds the authorship and publication of their work, it is thought that their writings probably were published by Marshall between the years 1783 and 1790.

Village School by "M. P." was a stubborn success despite the nauseating story it tells. Young Jacob Steadfast is taught his lessons in behavior by hearing the story of Ralph Breakclod, an unmitigated liar and thief. Among his other misdemeanors, he eats the pie he was to have delivered to his aged grandmother; and when he plays hooky from school, his excuse is a barefaced lie about having injured his leg. But, of course, no child could behave for long in this manner without receiving his just due. In good time, Ralph is run over by a vehicle. Because he had cried "Wolf" too often, his parents do not believe his claims of having sustained mortal wounds, and he dies within a week.

Jacob Steadfast, having learned about behavior from the tale of Ralph Breakclod, develops into a paragon of virtue. Although his truancy from school is justified because he had come upon a lamb with a broken leg which he had stopped to tend, he nevertheless is willing to take his punishment. Mr. Right, the squire, rewards Jacob with "a most entertaining book" called *The Memoirs of a Peg-Top,* a story by Miss Kilner, naturally. Mr. Right's school prizes always were "the pretty books from Mr. Marshall, the printer in London."[20] The Kilner girls were not above puffing their wares, for they were quite sanguine in their conviction that, through reading their stories, boys and girls would become fine, moral young men and women.

Mrs. Sarah (Kirby) Trimmer (1741-1810). The most militant savior of the young was Sarah Trimmer. Principles she had, and principles she expounded. There was nothing wishy-washy about Mrs. Trimmer. She knew what was good for children, but more to the point, she knew even better what was bad for them. She was well-acquainted with the literature that had been available for children in previous generations, and she looked upon most of it with stern disapproval. Mrs. Trimmer was a reactionary who harked back to the belief that children were innately sinful and must be rescued from this state.

With these ideas about children firmly grounded, it is understandable that she became a zealous follower of the Sunday School movement

---

[20]Ibid., p. 84.

for poor and illiterate children. This movement had been initiated by Robert Raikes, a prosperous newspaper owner, who also financed it. Inspired by Mrs. Barbauld's *Easy Lessons for Children,* Mrs. Trimmer developed a set of conversational lessons entitled *An Easy Introduction to the Knowledge of Nature.* "This discourse ranged from flax, to cabbages, to the dire consequences of a boy's eating green fruit, to mining in the bowels of the earth, to dairying, to beans."[21] It met with such great success that Berquin translated it into French for his youthful readers.

Mrs. Trimmer's crowning success was originally published as *Fabulous Histories,* 1786, but the title of later editions was *History of the Robins.* She not only wanted to redeem children from eternal damnation; she had her antenna out for parent approval, as well. In the preface to the *Robins,* the parent robins represent a loving father and mother of a human family. Although it was necessary that the little birds talk to one another, it was against Mrs. Trimmer's principles to permit children to have the pleasure of reading about talking animals. She must inform them that "birds really can't talk!" but that these stories must be regarded as fables which teach a lesson—and a moral one, naturally. Since Locke approved the fable as a vehicle for teaching, Mrs. Trimmer could use talking animals with impunity, too, and thus extricate herself rather neatly from the trap she had almost made for herself.

But talking birds or no talking birds, Mrs. Trimmer remained true to her conviction that fanciful, imaginative literature was false and immoral. Cinderella, in her considered opinion, was one of the worst stories ever written for children, depicting as it did the vilest of human passions—envy, jealousy, vanity, and hatred.[22]

Mrs. Sherwood (1775-1851). A runner-up to Mrs. Trimmer in that womanly art of creating horrifying and terrifying stories for children was Mrs. Sherwood. Of her prolific output of books, the most successful one was *The History of the Fairchild Family,* or the *Child's Manual being a Collection of Stories calculated to show the importance and effects of a religious education.* Here is implicit belief in the inherent evil in children. The first part of this *History* was published in 1818. It was continued in 1842, and the final installment was brought out with the aid of a married daughter in 1847. It is more than a hundred years too late to deplore the fact that it and Mrs. Sherwood's other compositions should ever have been attempted. The resilience of children is evidenced in the fact that they survived continued reprintings of this saga.

---

[21]Meigs, *Critical History,* p. 77.
[22]Ibid., p. 87.

In the introduction, Papa is giving a geography lesson, using a new globe which has just arrived. Muir, using his own character interpolations, describes the scene following the lesson.

> There upon, Lucy, little beast, pipes up, "papa, may we say some verses about mankind having evil hearts?" Permission being given, each of the three little monsters quotes a gloomy passage from Scripture. This leads to a homily from Papa on the complete and utter corruption of the human heart, whereupon little Henry caps all by exclaiming, Oh! I wish I could love the Lord Jesus Christ more than I do; but my wicked heart will not let me."[23]

There follow more than 540 pages of this stern, devastatingly sanctimonious piety.

Hannah More (1745-1833).   Like Mrs. Barbauld, Hannah More was in the satellite group revolving around the great Dr. Johnson. She was also a friend of Sir Joshua Reynolds, Horace Walpole, and the Garricks. Although she disapproved of the theater, she wrote a successful play, *Percy,* which was produced by Garrick.

Hannah More's early adult years were spent in a glittering, stimulating atmosphere of literary and theatrical people. But in the fourth decade of her life, the urban life palled, and she returned to Bristol. Here at Cowslip Green, she was joined by her older sisters who retired from their school for girls in Bristol.

The realization that there were no schools for the children of working people troubled Hannah More. She worried about their morals, too. Inspired by Sarah Trimmer and others, the More sisters threw themselves into the task of founding schools, using up their personal resources to obtain the buildings and grounds and to find teachers for the classes. Their first school at Cheddar met with success, and they renewed their energies in repeating these ventures many times.

Formidable workers that they were, they assumed the entire administration of these schools, planning the instruction, interviewing parents, and so forth. Here was a fertile field for Hannah More's writing talents. In this setting was born the *Cheap Repository Tracts,* in each of which was a story, a set of verses, and a sermon. Three of these tracts were issued each month for over three years—from 1792-1795—and sold millions of copies.

A typical example of these tracts is *The Shepherd of Salisbury Plain,* which follows the familiar pattern of moralizing so typical of the "womanly" writing of the time. Patience and fortitude in accepting the terrible trials and tribulations which poverty brings are extolled. Be industrious, thrifty, and content even though you may be starving, was the message conveyed.

---

[23]Muir, *English Children's Books,* p. 88.

The Shepherd, in numbers of long speeches, sets forth his situation to kindly Mr. Johnson, depicting his happy life with a wife crippled by rheumatism and five children in a house with leaky thatch and a broken chimney. When he is given a crown by the benevolent gentleman, he uses it to pay the doctor who tended his wife last winter when she was ill unto death. He fears that he can get no more medical aid until the debt is paid, nor will he buy meat for himself or the children until the doctor has had his due. By great good fortune the old clerk of the parish dies at this juncture and the shepherd gets his place and his weatherproof cottage, with "a large light kitchen" where he and his wife are to conduct a Sunday School.[24]

Though this good lady didn't believe in fanciful tales, she was masterful at the art of writing them. To her, it was axiomatic that virtue was rewarded and that evil was punished. Hannah More did not question this. She looked at the world through rose-colored glasses. Privilege, patronage, poverty, and inequality of opportunity and of material goods was everywhere apparent, but this well-meaning, literate, but really unintelligent author truly preferred to believe that the road leading from rags and hunger to riches and plenty was simply a matter of virtuous living. And so she wrote *Black Giles the Poacher, Tawny Rachel the Fortune Teller, The Happy Waterman,* and many other books.

Although she was abysmally narrow in her understanding of the sociological factors causing poverty, Hannah More was a crusader in promulgating the idea that the poor were worthy of education. She was not afraid to make them "unfit to be servants."[25]

Thomas Day (1748-1789). The History of Sandford and Merton epitomizes the "life is real, life is earnest" book which was the vogue of the period. It is realism at its most humorless peak. Muir sums it up in these words, "*The History of Sandford and Merton* is a feast of nausea. It is so ludicrously serious in its preposterous moralizings that in small doses it makes hilarious reading."[26]

It is true that Harry Sandford, the sturdy little farmer's boy, is also "the world's prize prig."

He had only once ever ill-treated a dumb creature, when he twirled a cockchafer fastened to a thread by a crooked pin. When his father told him that this was equivalent to the thrusting of a knife through his own hand he burst into tears, took the poor insect home, restored it to life by feeding it with fresh leaves, and then liberated it in the fresh air. Thereafter he would step out of his way to avoid hurting a worm, and would often go supperless to bed that he might feed the poor, starving robinredbreasts during periods of frost and snow.

---

[24]Meigs, *Critical History,* p. 81.
[25]Ibid., p. 81.
[26]Muir, *English Children's Books,* p. 91.

He preferred dry bread for his dinner to any kind of sweetmeat or fruit, and he knew that "we must only eat when we are hungry, and drink when we are thirsty . . . this was the way the Apostles did, who were all very good men."[27]

Naturally, the story would also have the weak (both physically and morally) character in the person of Merton, the poor little rich boy. These two stereotyped characters, plus Mr. Barlow, the local clergyman who becomes the preceptor, spend the whole first volume absorbed in making the statement in every way possible that "the rich do nothing and produce nothing, and the poor do everything that is useful."[28]

One cannot help wondering as Percy Muir does "why this masterpiece of sentimentality and bathos had such a long run." It was being read and reprinted more than one hundred years after the first printing. It seems unlikely that the children of that period were or wanted to be "smug little prigs." Perhaps their parents prolonged the book's popularity with the thought that Harry was a fine example of resourcefulness, self-denial, and all the other virtues rolled up into one. Perhaps there were no other choices of books for children. And so they read this one right up to the final paragraph which ends true to form:

> Tommy is taking leave of Harry to return home, and does so thus: To your example I owe most of the little good that I can boast; you have taught me how much better it is to be useful than rich or fine—how much more amiable to be good than to be great. Should I be ever tempted to relapse . . . I will return hither for instruction, and I hope you will receive me. Saying this, he shook his friend Harry affectionately by the hand, and, with watery eyes, accompanied his father home.[29]

Smug Harry is to have almost one hundred years of popularity before Thomas Bailey Aldrich's *The Story of a Bad Boy* appears, to be followed by Mark Twain's *The Adventures of Tom Sawyer* and *The Adventures of Huckleberry Finn*. Boys can be boys again—made of "snips and snails and puppy-dog tails."

Maria Edgeworth (1767-1849).   Maria was the second child of her famous father's twenty-two children. Richard Edgeworth was happily married four times, and Maria spent much of her life in helping to rear the numerous offspring of these marriages. Both Maria and her father were interested in educational methods, and they had the population at hand for experimentation. Richard Edgeworth had high regard for the theories of Thomas Day of Sandford and Merton fame. Maria was reared under this influence.

---

[27]Ibid., p. 92.
[28]Ibid., p. 93.
[29]Ibid., p. 93.

The Parent's Assistant was published by Maria Edgeworth in 1796. It was a companion to *Practical Education,* a book of essays which she had previously written in collaboration with her father. The original contained ten stories for children. It eventually grew to six volumes. Stories for younger children were culled out and published separately under the title, *Early Lessons.* "The Purple Jar" (see Chapter 2, p. 22), a story in the original series, is typical of Maria's writing. It was one of her favorites, and was popular with the reading public as well. Though Maria Edgeworth's stories are heavily moral and admonishing, her narrative style is far superior to that of her predecessors. She really did tell a story.

Samuel Goodrich (1793-1860). Writing under the name of Peter Parley, Samuel Goodrich was the American counterpart of British moralists, writing more than one hundred volumes of history, geography, science, and travel.

Tales of Peter Parley about America was published in 1827, *Tales of Peter Parley about Europe* in 1829, *Peter Parley's Evening Tales* in 1830, and on and on. One hundred seventy small volumes, selling five million copies, had been written by this prolific author by the year 1850.

Peter Parley, or rather Samuel Goodrich, was extremely literal. He thought that the lovable rascal, Puss in Boots, was a deceitful cheat, and that Jack the Giant-Killer was too bloody, (as, of course, he was, but what else could one do against a ferocious giant?). Humor and fancy were not part of the Peter Parley repertoire. He was a moralist who viewed children's books as vehicles for imparting fact and knowledge rather than as instruments of joy and recreation. Peter Parley tried to answer children's innate curiosity, but his "intellectual plum pudding" was not very rich and tasty."[30]

Early Magazines for Children

Journals for boys and girls were instrumental in the development of writing for children. Margaret Scott Gatty (1809-1873), as editor of *Aunt Judy's Magazine* (1866-1873), evidenced a flair for discovering new and talented writers and contributors. For example, *What the Moon Saw* by Hans Christian Andersen and *Alice in Wonderland* by Lewis Carroll were published by her.[31]

One of the most frequent contributors to *Aunt Judy's Magazine* was Mrs. Gatty's daughter, Juliana. The first installment of her serial, entitled *Mrs. Overtheway's Remembrances,* appeared in the first number of the magazine in 1866. As Mrs. Ewing, the wife of a major in the British

---

[30]Ibid., p. 144.
[31]Meigs, *Critical History,* p. 180.

Army, she also wrote stories about army life, among them "The Story of a Short Life" and "Jackanapes."

Though her fondness for deathbed scenes and other sentimentality are typical of her era, her books did please children and adults of the period because of the strong plots and the honest portrayal of children, flowers, and animals against the beauty of the English countryside.[32]

Among the magazines for boys were *Boy's World, Boys of England,* and the *Young Englishman's Journal.* These periodicals exploited the heroic deeds of such brave characters as Tom Merry and Jack Harkaway who performed their adventurous feats weekly.

In their prospectus, the editors of *Boys of England* stated, "Our aim is to entice you by wild and wonderful but healthy fiction."[33] There were many illustrations in these magazines, and the subscribers were enticed by schemes of distributing prizes such as watches, rabbits, and ponies.

Most of the writers of these forerunners of the modern serial and comic books used pseudonyms like Bracebridge Hemyng, Ralph Rollington, and Benchley Beaumont. They were Fleet Street hacks who wrote these yarns for boys as a strictly commerical enterprise. They had no illusions regarding the artistry of the material.

Other serial fiction at the time were the penny "bloods" which told "of exploits of famous highwaymen, from Dick Turpin to Springheel Jack."[34]

The school stories, among them *Tom Brown's School Days,* became successful at this time, too. Thomas Hughes based his story on his own reminiscences of his school days at Rugby. *Little by Little,* by F. W. Farrar, is another example of these school stories. The latter achieved great popularity at the time but did not have the staying power of Tom Brown.

The magazine serials and the school stories seem to have bridged the gap between the moralizing and admonishing of the preceding period and the writing of honest, realistic literature for boys and girls, literature which has a story to tell rather than a moral to preach.

The Juvenile Miscellany, the first magazine published in America that was really for children, was edited by Lydia Maria Child. "Mary Had a Little Lamb," written by Sarah Joseph Hale, appeared for the first time in this magazine.

Horace Scudder edited *The Riverside Magazine* for three years (1867-1870). Famous contributors included Hans Christian Andersen, Mary Mapes Dodge, Alice and Phoebe Cary, Edward Everett Hale, and

---

[32]Ibid., p. 186.
[33]Ibid., p. 186.
[34]Muir, *English Children's Books,* p. 112.

Frank R. Stockton. Illustrations were often contributed by Thomas Nast, E. B. Bensell, John LaFarge, and Winslow Homer. Of great importance for the development of taste in literature for children was the inclusion of articles on children's reading and children's choices.[35]

Lucy Larcom, the editor of *Our Young Folks,* also evidenced discriminating judgment in accepting material for publication. With J. T. Trowbridge as co-editor, she introduced children to Longfellow, Lowell, and Whittier. Aldrich's "The Story of a Bad Boy" was published in *Our Young Folks* in 1868 as was Charles Dickens' "The Magic Fishbone." The first part of *A Holiday Romance* appeared in the magazine in 1868, too. *The Peterkin Papers* by Lucretia Hale also made their first appearance under Lucy Larcom's editorship.

Our Young Folks was sold to Scribner's in 1874 and later became part of the most famous of all magazines for children, *St. Nicholas,* which first appeared under the editorship of Mary Mapes Dodge.

Dr. J. G. Holland, a director of Charles Scribner's Sons, conceived the idea of publishing a magazine for boys and girls with stories, poems, and articles which would meet the same high standards as Scribner's magazine for adults. Mrs. Dodge's interest in and understanding of young people, combined with her literary talent, made *St. Nicholas* the outstanding magazine for children of all time.

Mrs. Dodge firmly rejected didacticism, "Let there be no sermonizing . . . no spinning out of facts, no rattling of dry bones. . . . The ideal child's magazine is a pleasure ground."[36] Lucretia Hale's *The Peterkin Papers,* Joel Chandler Harris' *Uncle Remus Stories,* Kipling's *Toomai of the Elephants* and *Polly Cla,* (later part of *The Jungle Book*), and Howard Pyle's, *Jack Ballister's Fortunes* were among the fine literary experiences now available for boys and girls in the *St. Nicholas* magazine.

Mary Mapes Dodge set down an editorial policy at the beginning of her career as editor of *St. Nicholas,* a policy which she never changed. It became a guide, a challenge, and an inspiration for all present and future illustrators and publishers of children's books.[37]

> To give clean, genuine fun to children of all ages.
> To give them examples of the finest types of boyhood and girlhood.
> To inspire them with a fine appreciation of pictorial art.
> To cultivate the imagination on profitable directions.
> To foster a love of country, home, nature, truth, beauty, sincerity.
> To prepare boys and girls for life as it is.

---

[35]Meigs, p. 276.
[36]Ibid., p. 280.
[37]Ibid., p. 280.

To stimulate their ambitions—but along normally progressive lines.
To keep pace with a fast-moving world in all its activities.
To give reading matter which every parent may pass to his children unhesitatingly.[38]

QUESTIONS AND SUGGESTIONS

1. Read some stories from the Bible. Then read *The New-England Primer*. Compare and contrast their content.
2. Define the term "didactic" in relation to writing for children. Identify and discuss some of the modern children's books which seem to be written in this style. Compare them and discuss their appropriateness for children in terms of their literary quality and appeal to children's interests.
3. Why were the magazine stories written in England during the nineteenth century described as forerunners of the serial stories of the twentieth century? Select stories from several series such as the *Bobbsey Twins, Little Eddie Nancy Drew*, and the *Hardy Boys*. What do they have in common with the earlier magazine stories?
4. Choose some contemporary examples of children's literature which you believe exemplify the criteria set down by Mary Mapes Dodge in her editorial policy for the *St. Nicholas* magazine. Discuss the books in relation to these qualities and their appeal to children.

SELECTED CHAPTER REFERENCES

ADAMS, BESS PORTER. *About Books and Children*. New York: Holt, Rinehart & Winston, 1953.

DE VRIES, LEONARD. *Flowers of Delight*: An Agreeable Garland of Prose and Poetry. New York: Pantheon Books, 1966.

FIELD, MRS. E. M. *The Child and His Book*. 2d ed. Wells, Gardner, Darton and Co., 1892.

FOLMSBEE, BEULAH. *A Little History of the Horn Book*. Boston: The Horn Book, 1942.

FORD, PAUL LEICESTER. *The New-England Primer*. New York: Teachers College Press, Teachers College, Columbia University, 1962.

HUCK, CHARLOTTE S., and KUHN, DORIS YOUNG. *Children's Literature in the Elementary School*. 2d ed. New York: Holt, Rinehart & Winston, 1968.

MEIGS, CORNELIA; EATON, ANNE; NESBITT, ELIZABETH; and VIGUERS, RUTH HILL. *A Critical History of Children's Literature*. New York: Macmillan Co., 1953.

MUIR, PERCY. *English Children's Books: 1600-1900*. New York: Frederick A. Praeger, Publishers, 1954.

SLOANE, WILLIAM. *Children's Books in England and America in the Seventeenth Century*. New York: King's Crown Press, Columbia University Press, 1955.

[38]Ibid., p. 280.

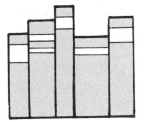

chapter 6

landmarks in literature
for children

Memorable Moments in Publishing

The notion that book printing for children exploded suddenly in 1744 with Newbery's publication of *A Little Pretty Pocket-Book* is an idea which has been abandoned by historians of children's literature. Two tiny volumes—both with the same title, *A Little Book for Little Children,*—may be found in the British Museum. One by Thomas White, dated 1703 (12th edition), warns against ballads and "foolish books" and fills the text with stories of religious martyrs. It also contains, of course, the alphabet in rhyme. For the letter "C":

> Children that make their parents hearts to Bleed:
> May live to have Children to revenge that deed.[1]

Early recreational reading indeed! But this first one was so intended. It was not published as a lesson book to be used in school; rather, it's purpose was to offer "light literature to bring joy to the hearts of their young readers." Of course these Puritan authors were undeniably sincere since they truly could not comprehend any greater joy than saving one's soul from perdition.

The other little book, by T. W. (still unknown), undated but with a woodcut frontispiece of Queen Anne, was probably printed about 1712, and has only twelve pages including the title page and frontispiece. Though this little book seems to have been designed to educate rather than "to recreate," it is the earliest book on record in English that approaches the problem from the point of view of the child, rather than the adult, a *landmark* of no mean importance.

The first text page, a letterpress representation of a hornbook, is followed by four pages of spelling lessons. The alphabet is illustrated

---

[1]Percy Muir, *English Children's Books: 1600-1900* (New York: Frederick A. Praeger, Publishers, 1954), p. 33.

with jingles—the first being "A was an Archer," the alphabetical rhyme
which had such strong staying power.

> A was an Archer, and shot at a frog,
> B was a Butcher and kept a great Dog,
> C was a Captain all covered with lace,
> D was a Drunkard with a red face;[2]

And so on. An object lesson follows:

> I saw a Peacock with a fiery Tail,
> I saw a Blazing Star that dropt down Hail,[3]

The last page is an advertisement for *The Child's Weeks Work*, Containing *Godly Verses, Riddles, Tables, Jests and Stories*, by William Ronksley, published in 1712.

From these beginnings, publishing for the young people in the population began to receive attention. Here was a virtually untapped market.

William Caxton (1421-1491). Publishing in the seventeenth and eighteenth centuries was not, historically speaking, a new business, William Caxton having run a thriving enterprise in 1484. The circumstances of Caxton's early life formed a background that greatly influenced his later life and subsequent fame. Born in "Kent in the Weeld" in 1421, he became at an early age a mercer's apprentice. After his apprenticeship, Caxton set up business in Bruges. While negotiating mercantile concessions, he met the Duchess Margaret, sister of King Edward IV of England, who as a patron of letters, employed copyists to produce manuscripts for her libraries at Malines and Binch. Her influence was a turning point in Caxton's life. With the aid of the Duchess, he was given access to important European libraries where he studied the French and Flemish romances and the new art of printing being introduced in Flanders from Germany. He began to translate into English some of the French romances in the Duchess' library.

And so it was that when he returned to England, the King offered patronage and friendship which enabled Caxton to set up his printing business in 1476 at the Red Pole in Westminster, near the Abbey. His first publication was Lord Rivers' translation, *Dictes and Sayengis of the Philosophers*.

Caxton's enterprising nature and his courage to act upon his convictions were the qualities which made him the one who was responsible for giving to English literature of the time a new face and style. He introduced the European romances to English readers and, not for-

---

[2]Ibid., p. 54.
[3]Ibid., p. 55.

getting the children, he published those rhymes and verses by an anonymous monk for the Lytyll Johns (1477), and a book of admonitions for the Lytyll Marys (1484). In 1483, he published *The Book Called Cathon* which was for "younge children in schole."

But the milestones in children's reading for which Caxton must be given just acclaim are *Morte d'Arthur* (1485), *Reynard the Fox* (Caxton's own translation), and of course, *Aesop's Fables* in 1484.

He worked to further the cause of English letters until his death, finishing his last translation the day before he died.

Nathaniel Crouch. Writing and compiling under the pseudonyms of Robert or Richard Burton, Nathaniel Crouch published books for children in the seventeenth century. His shilling books contained "useful and diverting" content including adventures, histories, riddles, pictures, and poetry.

Crouch knew the tastes of his reading public. He was the son of a tailor, and he knew the working classes' desire for inexpensive books. He aimed to please; he also aimed to acquire as many shillings as children could coax from their parents to purchase his books.

In 1691, he brought out R. B.'s *Youth's Divine Pastime* which consisted of thirty-six Bible stories in doggerel verse. Another publication was *Winter Evening's Entertainment*, in two parts. The first part was a group of short stories which he had copied before, but this time he gave them a new flavor by revamping them. The second part contained fifty illustrated riddles. Somehow or other, Crouch was able to fit two or three riddles to one picture, thus honing down the number of woodcuts to twenty-seven.

In modern jargon, Crouch would have been considered an "operator" in the pejorative sense of the word. He was a seventeenth century "wheeler and dealer" in the book trade, and one with no mean facility for plagiarism.

But Muir and Sloane, among other historians of children's literature, agree that though his books were cheap and hackneyed—far removed from standards of excellence—in his thirty-five years of publishing, he was significant in the evolution of book publishing for juveniles since he was the first to make an effort to provide "books of adventures, miracles, wonders, prodigies, and British history—popularizing knowledge, however sketchy, and making it accessible in inexpensive books."[4]

Chapbooks and Writing Sheets. Some early publishers seemed to have specialized in certain types of publishing, as for instance, the chapbook market. The principal publisher of these little penny books "suitable to everybody's taste and within everyone's price range" was

---

[4]William Sloane, *Children's Books in England and America in the Seventeenth Century* (New York: King's Crown Press, Columbia University Press, 1955), p. 5.

the firm of William and Cleur Dicey. Originally from Northhampton, the firm was called Raikes and Dicey, Northhampton. It was under the name C. Dicey, No. 4 Aldermary Churchyard, (later moved to Bow Churchyard) that most of the original chapbooks were published.

Early children's books are a truly elusive form of printed material. This may be understood when one realizes that, in earlier times when there were so few books to be traded and treasured, they eventually became literally worn out. The historian, then, may make the erroneous assumption that what does not survive, never was. There are few surviving children's books which offer clues to the period before John Newbery.

The printing of writing sheets, sometimes called school pieces, was one of the first known efforts to provide printed material especially for children. James Cole, in the early years of the eighteenth century, produced practical manuals for young students. These were gaily bordered sheets with space in the middle for the child's practiced script and were meant to be presented as gifts to parents on special occasions. They often had attractive colored pictures. Sometimes these pictures were grouped to tell a story. A comprehensive study of these writing sheets was published by Sir Ambrose Heal.[5]

Although the Perrault tales and the adaptations of *Gulliver's Travels* and *Robinson Crusoe* were available for young readers, and although chapbook publishers had catered to the juvenile clientele, it is Thomas Boreman who must be remembered as having been the first publisher whose avowed purpose was to specialize in publications for children. He did, however, publish other types of books. Because he seemed to have no identifiable successors, and because his records were not preserved, his work and efforts have been reconstructed from the publications which survived.

It is believed that Thomas Boreman was publishing in 1730. It appears that he was not a large-scale entrepreneur. Nothing seems certain about his activities except that he did indeed publish. Among his publications were *A Description of Three Hundred Animals; viz. Beasts, Birds, Fishes, Serpents and Insects* in 1730, and *A Description of a Great Variety of Animals and Vegetables* . . . especially for the entertainment of youth . . . in 1736.

But perhaps Boreman's *Gigantick Histories*[6] in nine volumes are truly the landmark which he laid down. Within these tiny books, three and a quarter by two and a quarter inches, perhaps the smallest ever made, were found historical and descriptive accounts of famous London buildings, among them the Guildhall, St. Paul's, Westminster, and The

---

[5]Sir Ambrose Heal, *The English Writing Masters and Their Copy Books* (Cambridge, England: Cambridge University Press, n.d.).
[6]See Chapter 1, p. 8.

Tower. These tiny volumes were bound in the gay Dutch floral boards associated with the name of Newbery.

The first volume was *The Gigantick History of the Two Famous Giants.* This is a legend rather than a true history of the two giants of the Guildhall, Corineus and Gogmogog. The preface to this first publication indicates Boreman's approach to juvenile publishing. "During the Infant Age ever busy and always enquiring, there is no fixing the attention of the Mind but by amusing it." Boreman further promises his young patrons if they buy his book:

> Then very soon
> I'll print another
> Which for Size
> Will be its Brother
> Such pretty Things
> It will contain
> You'll read it o'er
> And o'er again.[7]

Following this is a list of subscribers, which seemed to have been a major feature of Boreman's *Gigantick History* series. Among the eighty-five subscribers are the two giants (booksellers), who bought 100 copies each. The publishing imprint is Thos. Boreman, Bookseller, near the Two Giants in Guildhall. The record of multiple copies purchased by booksellers contained in his list of subscribers offers some evidence relating to Boreman's financial return. The books sold at fourpence each. Therefore, the total return to the publisher on the whole first edition in this series was estimated at approximately five pounds.

It is estimated that Boreman published approximately ten or eleven books for children, all of which he wrote himself. They had strong appeal because of their gay format and content as well as their little size and price. Boreman demonstrated that he was keenly aware of the qualities in a book that would capture the interest and fancy of children. It seems certain that his pioneer efforts had great influence on Newbery, who brought out an imitation of the *Gigantick Histories* in 1753 entitled *Descriptions of London.* Boreman's publications are described in an interesting monograph by William Stone.[8]

At about the same time, Mrs. Mary Cooper was successfully engaged in continuing her late husband's publishing business. In 1743, the year preceding Newbery's first book for children, she brought out her second edition of *The Child's New Plaything.* It contained, the traditional rhymes, such as "A Apple Pie," and some of the medieval tales of St.

---

[7]John Newbery, *A Little Pretty Pocket-Book* (New York: Harcourt, Brace & World, 1967), pp. 13, 14.

[8]William Stone, *The Gigantick Histories of Thomas Boreman* (Portland, Maine: Southworth Press), 1933.

George Fortunatus, Guy of Warwick, and Reynard the Fox sandwiched in with the spelling book lessons.

Mrs. Cooper's second book for children turned out to be a best seller of note. In the London Evening Post for 22 March, 1744, the following announcement appeared:

> This Day is publish'd. —Price 6d bound.
> *Tommy Thumb's Song Book* for all little
> Masters and Misses to be sung to them
> by their Nurses till they can sing
> them themselves. By Nurse Lovechild.[9]

This is the first known publication of nursery rhymes.

These earlier publishers of children's books set the style for John Newbery who truly became a "giant" in the business. According to Thwaite, Meigs, and other historians, the times seemed most fortuitous for Newbery to pick up the ideas so well-begun by Boreman, Cooper, and others. Authors were becoming less dependent upon patrons, more often dealing directly with the book publisher and the seller.

Books likely to gain a profit from a wide sale were in demand by publishers in the eighteenth century mainly because there was a wider reading populace. Many ladies of fashion, parents, merchants, and tradesmen were now reading for the sheer pleasure of reading. A growing interest in education during the age of enlightenment had influenced the development of a widespread practice of teaching reading, even to the poor children in some of the new charity schools. Though reading the Bible was still considered to be the most important use of reading, and even the most important reason for learning how to read, other kinds of books were becoming more in demand.

John Newbery (1713-1767). It was at this time of increased interest in books and reading that John Newbery appeared upon the scene. He was born in Berkshire in 1713. His parents were farmers of little means. After some formal education, he went to Reading where he became apprenticed to William Ayres, a printer who also published the *Reading Mercury.* By 1737, a William Carnan came into possession of this printing business and moved it to the Market Place in Reading where it flourished. After Carnan's death, Newbery married Mrs. Carnan, in 1739, and thus became the stepfather of John, Thomas, and Anna-Maria Carnan. Meanwhile, Newbery's imprint began to appear on the paper which was now being published at the Bible and Crown, Market Place, in Reading.

The city of Reading became too small for Newbery's vigorous energy and talents. In 1745, we find him (after short terms at two other addresses) doing business in London at St. Paul's Churchyard in a shop,

---

[9]Newbery, *Pretty Pocket-Book,* p. 17.

The Bible and Sun, which was to become so celebrated. John Carnan remained at Reading to carry on the business which had been started by his father.

Newbery's greatest talent probably lay in his vigorous and bold business acumen rather than in literary scholarship and sensitivity. He was an indefatigable promoter of whatever might be included among his expanding enterprises. His activities were varied in the early days in Reading and continued to be in London. The range of his interests is indicated by this advertisement which appeared in the *Reading Mercury* on September 29, 1740:

> John Newbery at the Bible and Crown in the Market Place, Reading, keeps a wholesale warehouse, and furnishes shopkeepers with all sorts of haberdashery goods (such as threads, tapes, bindings, ribbons, pins, needles, etc.) as cheap as in London. And any person by sending a letter to him will be as well served as if they came in person.[10]

Quack medicines were part of Newbery's stock in trade, too. Dr. Hooper's Female pills were among the early paliatives peddled by him, and later, he did a thriving trade in Dr. James' Fever Powder. He missed no opportunity to increase sales and to make the public aware of the powder's efficacy. He was not above cleverly puffing his books with references to his patent medicines. Muir cites the instance in *Goody Two-Shoes* when Margery's father did not survive the fever which befell him because Dr. James' Fever Powder was not available.

Welsh offers examples of Newbery's practice of padding his publications by inserting situations in his books in which a character might excuse himself to pause for a while in Mr. Leake's shop in Bath to read one of the Newbery books, or when

> another young prig deservedly christened Theophilus bewailed to his father the ill fortune of those benighted youngsters whose parents could not afford to purchase them such a nice gilded library as that obtainable from the good friends of all children in St. Paul's Churchyard, and so on.[11]

Newbery typified the rising mercantile class of the time. Children may be forever grateful that his interest was captured by the idea of publishing books especially for juveniles. It is said that he did indeed have a deep and sincere affection for children. He was much influenced by Locke's theories of education and his statements concerning the lamentable lack of easy, pleasant books from which children might learn. Locke also firmly believed that strong character and virtuous behavior were more important qualities than the mere learning of lessons.

---

[10]Ibid., p. 30.
[11]Cited in Muir, *English Children's Books*, p. 66.

And so Newbery published moral lessons for children in a manner which he thought would be pleasing to them. Self-control, prudence, moderation, rational judgment, honesty, industry, and benevolence are consistently fostered in the content of his books.

Though A *Little Pretty Pocket-Book* can make no claim to a "Newbery Award" for distinguished literary quality in children's writing, its style did bring humor to children's books, and the lessons and morals which are carefully imbedded in the text are often done in verse or game format. The alphabet is taught in gay verse style with the letters being used for pagination—much more fun than numbers!

The 'agreeable letters' of Jack the Giant-Killer to Master Tommy and Miss Polly, though packed with admonitions about being a "good boy" or "good girl," are palatable because of the personalized style of address. (If Jack the Giant-Killer bothered to write you a letter in a small, gay, floral-covered book, wouldn't you read it with great avidity?) As Jack soothes the little boys by telling them of the good reports he has received from their nurses, he is, in fact, listing all of the behaviors from cleanliness to godliness which are fostered and cherished in the society. And to wit, the Red and Black Ball is part and parcel of the bargain.

> And, while you behave so well, you shall never want Play I assure you. But then, my dear Tommy, in order that you may be as good as possible, I have also sent you a Ball, the one Side of which is Red, and the other Black, and with it ten pins; and I must insist upon making this Bargain, that your Nurse may hang up the Ball by the String to it, and for every good action you do a Pin shall be stuck on the Red Side, and for every bad Action a Pin shall be stuck on the Black Side. And when by doing good and pretty Things you have got all the ten Pins on the Red Side, then I'll send you a Penny, and so I will as often as all the Pins shall be fairly got on that Side. But if ever the Pins be all found on the Black Side of the Ball, then I'll send a Rod, and you shall be whipt as often as they are found there. But this, my Dear, I hope you'll prevent by continuing a good Boy, that every body may still love you, as well as Your Friend, Jack the Giant-Killer. P. S. When you are tired with playing, I have added, for your further Amusement, a Collection of pretty Songs, which your Nurse will take Care to Teach you; and I must insist on your getting them perfectly, because the Knowledge of these Songs will recommend you to the Favour of all the Gentlemen and Ladies of England who sing in that Manner.[12]

The Aesop's Fables and proverbs which conclude the Pocket-Book are perhaps the gayest entries. The fables are told in simple verse, and the heavy moralizing is substituted by Jack the Giant-Killer's briefer and more engaging interpretations.

---

[12]Newbery, *Pretty Pocket-Book*, pp. 65-66.

THE WOLF AND THE KID

As the Goat went to brouze,
Thus her Charge did begin;
Be advis'd, my dear Kid,
And let nobody in.
The Wolf hearing this
For Admittance did try,
But the Kid answer'd, No;
I'll not trust you, not I.[13]

TO MASTER TOMMY, OR MISS POLLY

You see, my Dear, the little Kid, by taking her Parent's Advice, preserved her own Life; for had she been so wicked as to have neglected what the Goat (her Mother) said to her, and had open'd the Door, the Wolf would certainly have torn her to pieces. Take care therefore to do always as your Papa and Mamma, or your Master and Mistress shall direct you, and you'll oblige, Your old Friend, Jack the Giant-Killer.[14]

Newbery later published a full volume of Aesop's Fables assigning authorship to Abraham Aesop, Esquire.

All the Newbery books were issued under pseudonyms, invented characters, or simply anonymously. Newbery's association with Oliver Goldsmith is well-documented, and it is *assumed* that Goldsmith authored some of the books for children. Christopher Smart, the poet who married his stepdaughter, Anna-Maria Carnan, is also *assumed* to have written some of the Newbery books, or parts of them.

When John Newbery turned his attention to children's books, he was very careful with all details—recruitment of authors, titles, prices, bindings, and pictures, as well as the advertising of his wares, a phase for which he had a particular talent.[15] For instance, Nurse Truelove's *New Year's Gift* (1760) was "designed as a present for every little boy who would become a great man and ride upon a fine horse, and to every little girl who would become a great woman and ride in a Mayor's gilt coach." Nurse Truelove's *Christmas Box*, subtitled *The Golden Plaything for Little Children*, (1750), cost only one penny.[16]

Twenty years passed between the publication of the *Pocket-Book* and *Goody Two-Shoes*. *The History of Little Goody Two-Shoes* turned out to be a "best seller" of the day. What would be considered a grossly melodramatic soap opera type story today was published by Newbery with no embarrassment at its having been taken from a manuscript

---

13Ibid., p. 114.
14Ibid., p. 114.
15Ibid., p. 65.
16Muir, p. 66.

found in the Vatican. The original manuscript purportedly had been illustrated by Michelangelo.[17]

By 1765, Newbery had truly established himself as a successful and prosperous bookseller. Along with the children's books for which he has achieved everlasting fame, he published such notable works as Johnson's *Idler* and Goldsmith's *Citizen of the World*. He also published books about medicine in addition to merely selling remedies.

Dr. James' Fever Powder continued to be a profitable item, so much so that it enabled Newbery to send his son, Francis, to Oxford. Francis was the one who eventually continued with this facet of the business after his father's death.

In 1767, after John Newbery's death, his stepson, Thomas Carnan, took over the original business. Newbery's nephew, also named Francis, moved to the top of Ludgate Hill at the Corner of St. Paul's Churchyard and carried on a rival business until his death in 1780. Francis' widow, Elizabeth Newbery, continued to run this business.

It appears from the records that, after Thomas Carnan's death in 1788, a grandson of John Carnan, Francis Power, was in charge of the Newbery enterprise. Sometime in the 1790's, all of the businesses were transferred to Mrs. Elizabeth Newbery. It is here that the Newbery imprint ends. John Harris, Mrs. Newbery's manager, took over at the famous corner of St. Paul's Churchyard, and the old Bible and Sun premises were vacated. From this point on, the John Harris imprint supplants the Newbery imprint. As a result of his close association with the Newbery enterprises, Harris, and his son succeeding him, continued to publish in the Newbery tradition the books which appealed to "the little Masters and Mistresses."[18]

John Harris. When he took over the Newbery enterprises, John Harris was full of ideas which he had not been permitted to try out as Mrs. Newbery's manager. His use of metal engravings in place of woodcuts was an effective innovation. He is also noted for his boldness in the use of color in his publications.

Two of his many publications were particularly memorable and have easily weathered the tests of time. On June 1, 1805, *Old Mother Hubbard* made her appearance, with the initials of a Miss Sarah Martin on the title page. Engravings were made from Miss Martin's drawings. *The Comic Adventures of Old Mother Hubbard and Her Dog* became an immediate success. It sold thousands of copies and was reprinted repeatedly from that time on. Whether Miss Martin did in fact write this loved adventure, or whether the character was Old Dame

17Ibid., p. 66.
18M. F. Thwaite, "John Newbery and his first book for children," introductory essay to Newbery, John. *A Little Pretty Pocket-Book.* (New York: Harcourt, Brace & World, 1967), pp. 1-4.

Trot originated by Elizabeth Sandham in 1803, as Iona and Peter Opie suggest,[19] seems of little importance. *The Butterfly's Ball* was another great publishing triumph for Harris.

John Harris had wisdom and great sensitivity in his selections of books which children would enjoy. His greatest gift to children's literature was the omission of the repetitive and incessant admonitions about manners and morals which had characterized most of the books published for children during the eighteenth century. His works were truly a landmark on the road to reading for pleasure.

Isaiah Thomas (1749-1831). Often referred to as Newbery's American counterpart, Isaiah Thomas of Worcester, Massachusetts had, like Newbery, a keen sense of salesmanship. He understood people—what they would *enjoy* and what they would *buy.* The Locke influence was seeping into the American colonies during the eighteenth century. Concentration on escape from the eternal pains of hell was slackening. Emphasis was moving toward the acquisition of those behavioral traits which led to a virtuous life. It was believed that this way of life, in turn, would bring success. Although many historians suggest that this literature for children (if it may be so dignified by the name) led to the development of self-righteous little prigs, it was the popular mode of the day.

Isaiah Thomas was apprenticed at an early age—perhaps when he was only six years old—and he may have set up a broadside, *The Lawyer's Pedigree*, before he could even read it.[20]

It is believed that, during the Revolutionary War, he came into possession of a number of the Newbery books, among them *Goody Two-Shoes* and *Mother Goose.* After the war, at a time when imports were difficult to obtain, Thomas simply took it upon himself to publish some of the Newbery books under his own imprint. Piracy, thievery, dishonest practices? In modern times, yes. But in those earlier publishing days, licensing and copyright laws were not regularized sufficiently to protect publishers from such practices. From chapbook days on, a publisher often brought out a book that had already been printed by another publisher. Since books were still scarce in a growing market, this plagiaristic practice apparently did not create the disastrous feuds and entanglements which would evolve in modern times.

The years between 1785 and 1788 seem to have been Thomas' greatest period of concentration on children's publications. During his childhood he had enjoyed Newbery's books. As a result, he packaged his publications in the Newbery style—bindings of marble and embossed

---

[19]Iona and Peter Opie, *The Oxford Book of Nursery Rhymes* (Oxford: The Clarendon Press, 1951), pp. 319-21.
[20]Cornelia Meigs, et al. *A Critical History of Children's Literature* (New York: Macmillan Co., 1953), p. 130.

paper, and covers of Dutch flowered papers. Thomas was most selective, however, in his Newbery pilfering. That he had an unerring sense of what would be popular is attested to in the titles which he printed—*Mother Goose, Nurse Truelove's New Year's Gift,* and others.

Even his advertising was in the manner of Newbery. The personalized touch was much in evidence. In his 1786 publication of *Nurse Truelove's New Year's Gift,* Mrs. Williams talked about "Plumb Cake from Turkey" and "candied sweetmeats from the East Indies." Thomas also had her prescribe an "I. Thomas reading list" to the pupils in her college. Free gifts of the *Webster Spelling Book* which he printed in multiple editions, and some of "the other pretty little books which are sold by I. Thomas" were offered as bribes for being the dutiful and submissive student of the New Testament.

The American I. Thomas did not search for writing talent in his own country nor did he attempt writing on his own. It appears that he did execute some rather crude woodcuts and that perhaps he wrote some verses for his earlier broadsides. He seems to have had a great affection and attachment for the Newbery books. (Or was it that they had proved their worth?) At any rate, after going through the best of Newbery, he seems to have turned his attention to other endeavors.

Hugh Gaine (1727-1807). Names of authors of books in the earlier days are far more elusive than those of publishers. Beginning somewhat earlier than Thomas, in a shop called the Bible and Crown at Hanover Square, in New York City, Hugh Gaine printed the Newbery books and patterned his business after the style of Newbery to some extent. He also sold remedies, and he used Newbery's puffing methods in his books to advertise them. He printed books for adults and children, but he also imported many books from England. The style and grace of his format and print have been considered outstanding for the times.[21]

Other publishers who should be mentioned as being important influences in the growing movement of providing books for children are Mohlon Day of New York, Thomas and John Fleet of Boston, William Charles of Philadelphia, and Benjamin and Jacob Johnson in partnership with Benjamin Warner in Philadelphia. The list of their publications is extensive. Chapbooks, *The Divine Songs of Isaac Watts, Mrs. Barbauld, Maria Edgeworth,* and many Newbery books were among them. Of course, we have met Thomas Fleet earlier in this text and know that he and Mother Goose are inextricably entangled in the confusions of the origin of the name for those favorite of all rhymes, the Mother Goose Rhymes.

---

[21]Ibid., p. 133.

Memorable Moments in Illustrating

Illustration in children's books has had a gradual evolution. It is only in the twentieth century, as graphic processes have become refined and less expensive, that we have had a magnificent and colorful artistic explosion in children's books.

Bestiaries, tales which combined the features of natural history and of Aesop's fables were written by monks from the fifth century onward and were used as vehicles to teach spiritual truths. The illuminated drawings of these fabulous creatures delighted the young scholars who rarely had the opportunity to hold the precious manuscripts in their own hands. An English bestiary of the twelfth century contains pictures of "The Panther Attracting Animals with Its Fragrant Breath," "The Yale (or Eale) with Movable Horns," and "The Mother Bear Licking Her Cubs into Shape," among the dragons, unicorns, and other unlikely mythical beasts which imagination and fancy created.

Even after the invention of printing, the idea of illustrations in books made very slow headway. Caxton's *Aesop's Fables,* printed in 1484, contained 185 woodcuts. This was certainly a landmark in the field of book illustration.

But the art in early books for children was fairly primitive. Pictures were usually printed from rather coarsely cut wood blocks. When these were printed on cheap papers, the results were often difficult to interpret. This is particularly true of many of the surviving examples which tend to be reprints rather than the originals. But to young readers of the time, the illustrations interspersed with the text were pleasant, gay, and often amusing.

The chapbooks carried crude illustrations which made the stories "come alive" for the readers. As chapbooks were gradually accepted, regularized, and issued freely by publishers as being suitable for juveniles, the various crucial and lively experiences of Tom Thumb, Dick Whittington, and all the other characters in the "Famous Histories" were engraved and printed.

Thomas Bewick (1753-1828). The first artist who devoted his time exclusively to illustrating books was Thomas Bewick. In 1767, he was apprenticed to a Newcastle engraver of doorplates, teaspoons, letterheads, and sundries. Woodcuts, used at the time for broadsides and chapbooks, were considered less important commercial properties. These were turned over to young Thomas who delighted in experimenting with the materials. He devised a new type of graving tool and developed the use of the "white line" and the end-grain block to achieve delicate effects. It was due to his artistry that the woodcuts regained popularity for illustrating books.

Thomas Bewick became a partner in the Newcastle firm, and his younger brother, John, was taken on as an apprentice. The older Bewick, using his experience in making cuts of animals for alphabet books and books of fables, made "A Pretty Book of Pictures for Little Masters and Misses" or *Tommy Trip's History of Beasts and Birds*. Empathy with the pleasures of childhood are evident in the skill with which these cuts are executed.

The Select Fables of Aesop and Others was illustrated by the brothers Bewick and came out in 1784. In the year 1792, another juvenile, *The Looking Glass for the Mind*, an adaptation of Berquin's *L'Ami des Enfants*, was published, John Bewick's figures of children with their lace collars and tiny coat-tails lent an intimacy and appeal that captivated the readers.

Illustration from John Bewick's *Looking Glass for the Mind*. Reprinted by permission of The Horn Book, Inc. from *Illustrators of Children's Books, 1744-1945*, compiled by Bertha E. Mahony et al.

A study of Bewick's woodcuts reveals integrity, humor, and sensitivity to beauty. That he possessed the skill to capture these qualities in line and space and engrave them on wood was indeed a gift supreme to the children of the time. It was also an extremely important landmark to guide his successors.

William Blake (1757-1827). Already cited in the poetry chapter of this book for his *Songs of Innocence*, William Blake must be mentioned among the artists, too. Though he remained a solitary and aloof figure in those early years of writing, publishing, and illustrating, his consummate artistry in developing the harmonious relationship between illustrations and words in the original editions of *Songs of Innocence* and *Songs of Experience* are truly landmarks in the illustration of children's books. The fact that he ground and mixed the colors on a piece of marble, with carpenter's glue for a binder, that he applied the colors and taught his wife how to take off impressions and help tint the twenty-seven three by five inch plates for *Songs of Innocence* is indeed remarkable.

George Cruikshank (1792-1878). The streets of London with their familiar but changing sights and smells and people were part of George Cruikshank's bone and marrow. In Dickens' *Sketches by Boz,* and in *London Characters, Mornings in Bow Street, Sunday in London,* and many other books illustrated by him, Cruickshank caricatured his beloved city and its people with the exaggerated style and warm humor for which he is remembered today.

His bold imagination and originality are forever captured in the 1823 translation of the Grimm's Fairy Tales. The spirit of these tales has perhaps never again been as successfully captured in pictures. "The Elves and the Shoemaker" was Cruikshank's all time favorite illustration of those lovely characters.

Among Cruikshank's memorable illustrations are those which accompany the dialogue of the *Tragical Comedy or Comical Tragedy of Punch and Judy.* Written by Payne Collier, it was published about 1828.

The *Comic Alphabet* offered an opportunity for Cruikshank to indulge himself in some sheer fun. With his Nightmare, and the Very Unpleasant predicament of the fat man evading the bull, he took care of N, U, and V as hilariously as he did the rest of the letters.

Another volume of this prolific illustrator's artistry, one to be remembered, is *The Cruikshank Fairy Book.* This originally appeared as *The Fairy Library* and contained four old tales—"Hop-o-My-Thumb," "Puss in Boots," "Jack and the Beanstalk," and "Cinderella." These are happy stories, and the fancy of the illustrator matches the fancy of the tales—Jack riding off on the harp, Hop being pursued by the giant ogre, and so forth. Happy, gay pictures, done in a happy, gay manner by a happy artist, surely.

John Tenniel (1820-1914). Although he contributed memorable cartoons to *Punch* between the years 1850 and 1900, it was John Tenniel's illustrations for Lewis Carroll's *Alice in Wonderland* (1865) and *Through the Looking-Glass* (1872) which placed him in the children's book illustrators' hall of fame. Here we have two men of differing talents, Lewis Carroll and John Tenniel, who together were able to create the oneness of picture and text which William Blake had earlier achieved.

Both had strong feelings and opinions about the rightness, the artistry of the results. Lewis Carroll worried about Tenniel's interpretations. He felt that Alice should not have too much crinoline and that the white knight, though bewhiskered, must not look too old.[22] Tenniel, on the other hand, suggested the omission of the last of Carroll's thirteen manuscript chapters which, in his judgment, did not match the quality of the other chapters. The chapter contained a "wasp in a wig" episode, an idea which to Tenniel seemed incapable of artistic expression.

The Wonderland created in words by Carroll was so faithfully and exquisitely reproduced in pictures by Tenniel that it is not surprising that he became "all drawn out" and never illustrated books again. Perhaps he knew that such perfection could never be duplicated.

John Tenniel: The Queen's Croquet-Ground, from *Alice's Adventures In Wonderland* by Lewis Carroll. Reproduced by permission of The Horn Book, Inc.

Edmund Evans and Frederick Warne. Three illustrators of children's books, Walter Crane, Randolph Caldecott, and Kate Greenaway, were influenced and motivated by Edmund Evans, a pioneer in color printing. At his Raquet Court Press off Fleet Street in London, Evans was waging a one man crusade against the rather crude and vulgar illustrations in the children's books of the time. Other printers and publishers thought the illustrations were good enough. "If the public will buy, why bother?" was their attitude.

And to Frederick Warne must go the credit for being willing to publish books with better color. He published Crane's first nursery

---

[22]Bertha Mahony et al., *Illustrators of Children's Books, 1744-1945* (Boston: Horn Book, 1947), p. 49.

picture books, *The House that Jack Built, Dame Trot and Her Comical Cat,* and the *History of Cock Robin and Jenny Wren.* Figures in bright colors were placed on solid black or blue backgrounds in the illustrations in these books. They were engraved by Edmund Evans with the most exquisite precision and artistry.

Walter Crane (1856-1915). Both the quantity and the quality of Walter Crane's work contributed to children's pleasure. His illustrations were characterized by their fine design, boldness of outline, and the use of strong, primary, almost primitive color. *The Absurd ABC, Puss in Boots, The Baby's Alphabet,* and *Sleeping Beauty,* were a few in a long list of his titles. The mood and tone of these old tales were heightened and enhanced by Crane's varied use of oranges, blues, and browns.

Bertha Mahony considered Walter Crane's *The First of May* one of his finest works. In this project, he worked with a Mr. Wise who was creating a fairy masque. Drawings of fairies, elves, children, shepherds, the Queen of the May, birds, insects, and beasts were made in pencil and then reproduced by a photogravure process which retained their delicate effect. Since no type was considered fine enough to blend with the designs, all the words were hand-lettered by Crane.

Obviously, the cost of reproducing this book was great, a fact which necessitated its being published in only a limited edition. It is, therefore, not so well known as some of his other books.

Randolph Caldecott (1846 1886). At an early age, Randolph Caldecott evidenced a strong interest in art activities. By the time he was six years old, he drew, modeled, and carved animals in a variety of media. But art as a profession was frowned upon by his father, and so, at the age of fifteen, he was steered into the banking business at Whitchurch in Shropshire. But fortunately for Caldecott (and for the world), he lived a few miles out in the country where he absorbed the rustic life after work and on holidays. Just as Cruikshank was intensely observant and aware of the city sights of London, so Caldecott was sensitive to and observant of the many facets of country life, such as markets, fairs, and hunts. He went to London in 1872 and subsequently became an illustrator for the *London Graphic.*

Caldecott is well known for his illustrations of Washington Irving's *Old Christmas* which was concerned with old-time English country life. This assignment suited Caldecott's taste perfectly, since his love of English country life had never abated. J. D. Cooper, the engraver who so carefully worked with him, was given due honors with Caldecott in the foreword.

Caldecott's picture books, started in 1877 or 1878, are the works, of course, for which he has achieved such great and lasting fame. The influence of Edmund Evans, the printer, was in evidence with Caldecott as it was with Walter Crane.

Caldecott's natural good humor and ebullient spirits seem to have been set free in his picture books. Animals, horses, children, the whole English countryside, are set forth in full panoply. *The Diverting History of John Gilpin* was the first of the series and was followed by a host of others, among them *The Fox Jumps over the Parson's Gate, The Frog He Would A-Wooing Go, The House that Jack Built, The Queen of Hearts, Ride a Cock Horse,* and so on. These were usually published singly, had paper covers, and sold for a shilling. Later, several were bound together into *Picture Book No. 1, Picture Book No. 2,* and the *Panjandrum Picture Book.* After a time, all the toy books, as they were called, were bound together into a large edition called *The Complete Collection of Pictures and Songs* with a preface by Austin Dobson.

"Ride a Cock-Horse to Banbury Cross" from *The Panjandrum Picture Book* by Randolph Caldecott. Repinted by permission of Frederick Warne & Co., Inc.

"The Queen of Hearts" from *Randolph Caldecott's Picture Book* (No. 2). Reprinted by permission of Frederick Warne & Co.. Inc.

The Caldecott Award which presently is conferred annually to the illustrator of the most distinguished children's book of the year, is well-named, indeed. Caldecott's own delightful picture books represent the innovation of an important trend in children's books. Here, for the first time, we have a tremendous creative talent in craftsmanship being expended in the making of lovely picture-reading for young children. The sensitive charm and unfailing good humor of this remarkable artist

"Sing a Song of Sixpence" from *Randolph Caldecott's Picture Book* (No. 2). Reprinted by permission of Frederick Warne & Co., Inc.

shine through his drawings and speak out from them today as they did when he created them.

Kate Greenaway (1846-1901). The name, Kate Greenaway, and pictures of English gardens seem to be inextricably combined. Bright, healthy, chubby children inhabit these gardens, and a gay, happy, "all's well with the world" mood emanates from the pages.

Kate Greenaway's father was a wood engraver whose illustrations appeared in early editions of *Punch* and in the *Illustrated London News.* Kate spent many holidays on her great-aunt's farm near Nottingham. It was here that she grew to love the gardens and the flowers which she depicts with such joy.

Simple verses accompany her drawings. Since the Greenaway talent lay in drawing rather than in writing, the verses merely create the framework for her children, whether they are picking daisies, playing games, or engaging in any of the other joyful activities of childhood.

Her first picture book was *Under the Window,* published in 1878. *Marigold Garden* followed in 1885. Though she illustrated two books written by Charlotte Yonge, and some by other authors, she preferred to choose her own vehicles. In 1881, she published an illustrated *Mother*

Goose that had all the Greenaway charm, and also *A Day in a Child's Life,* a book of songs set to music by Miles Foster.

A friend whose counsel, praise, and criticism she welcomed was John Ruskin. Though he chided her on the "prettiness" of her drawings and demanded more realistic representation from her, he respected her honesty, sincerity, and the truly deep affection she had for the children in her reading audience.

Although the Greenaway illustrations and verses might be described as light, gay, frothy, and not very true to the way things really are, her work found favor with adults and children alike. Perhaps it was the respite from the workaday world, the pleasant, playful aura that she projected which attracted and captured the Greenaway reading audience.

Little Miss Muffet,
Sat on a tuffet,
Eating some curds and whey;
There came a great spider,
And sat down beside her,
And frightened Miss Muffet away.

A page from Kate Greenaway's *Mother Goose.* Reprinted by permission of Frederick Warne & Co., Inc.

Memorable Moments in Writing

BOOKS THAT HAVE LIVED

Pilgrim's Progress. The young readers of the seventeenth century found in *Pilgrim's Progress* (1676) a story packed with travel and action. The places are clear and real, and the dangers arise with satisfying frequency to hold the reader in wrapt attention. For mature readers, the story is an allegory—but not so to children. For them, it is a real journey covering real miles.

John Bunyan (1628-1685) was a victim of the fluctuating positions of the church during his early years. The changing English Church of the time, from Catholicism to Protestantism, back to Catholicism, and then again to Protestantism, was confusing for many. It was very troubling to a sensitive thinker like John Bunyan.

The Puritan movement was a development which had as its purpose what its name implies—to purify—to cleanse the church of all of its impurities and corruption. Bunyan was a godly man in the true sense of the word. He was convinced that the simple, good life was the way to an understanding of eternal truths and the way to salvation. So firm was he in his beliefs that he felt compelled to preach about them to others. This he did, though preaching without a license was a criminal offense.

Because of this practice, Bunyan was in and out of prison much of the time. In prison, he wrote as assiduously as he preached when he was a free man. *Pilgrim's Progress* was created during one of his prison terms and published in 1676. John Bunyan would have been astonished had he known that his powerful allegorical story of man's earthly search for salvation and eternal life was to be preempted by children as an adventure story. But he had contributed a creative literary experience for the young reader at a time when such literary experiences were virtually non-existent.

Gulliver's Travels. Another allegory intended as a serious book for adults but adopted by children as entertaining reading resulted from the creative talent of Jonathan Swift (1667-1745). This book, of course, was *Gulliver's Travels.* It, too, is a tale of journeys to strange and distant places with shipwrecks and struggles for survival in the manner of Robinson Crusoe. The island of Lilliput, the country of the Brobdingnagians and the events which happened in these places have provided amusing and entertaining reading for the generations of young people who have followed Lemuel Gulliver in his travels.

One of the most brilliant men of his day, Jonathan Swift was known also to be one of the most unhappy. Power and prestige eluded him at every turn. When he was banished to Ireland for fourteen years, he revived the writing project which had been started so enthusiastically by Alexander Pope, Thomas Parnell, John Arbuthnot, John Gay, and himself—all members of the Scriblerus Club. His plan was to collaborate on a book which would ridicule and burlesque education through a main character—an educated dunce to be named Martin Scriblerus.

Interest in the plan soon subsided, and as Swift reminisced about it in Ireland, he decided to expand the idea to include, not only the inadequacy of education, but also the corruptness and incompetence found among many persons who held political power. In the new version, Martin Scriblerus not only changed his name, but he had a personality change as well. From the blundering, inept, educated fool, Martin, he was changed to Lemuel Gulliver, the "average man," whose adventures underscored the cruelties, inconsistencies, and vanities of the aristocrats of England. This was the means which Jonathan Swift chose to express his hostility toward a segment of society which had managed to frustrate him in seeking his goals.

Published anonymously in 1726, the reception Gulliver's Travels was given surprised the author; it boomeranged. England laughed and enjoyed the book. It has continued to entertain to the present day.

Robinson Crusoe. The name, Alexander Selkirk, has almost faded into oblivion, while that of Robinson Crusoe is known to all literate people. And yet, if Daniel Defoe had not met the sailor, Selkirk, and heard his yarn, hours of reading pleasure and dramatic role playing would have been lost to generations of young people.

Selkirk's adventure was as a castaway marooned on a deserted island off the coast of Chile. His story and the ingenuity he used to keep himself alive and fairly comfortable for four long years before being rescued was printed in various accounts and became the talk of London. But in time, other events captured the public interest, and Selkirk's saga was forgotten. But Daniel Defoe did not forget.

Daniel Defoe (1659-1731) became involved in the religious and political controversies of his time. In a pamphlet entitled *A Short Way with Dissenters,* he censured the High Church party and found himself placed in the pillory for three hours in public humiliation. He was arrested and given a long term in Newgate prison. This caused his tile-making business to suffer irreparably, and he was reduced to very dire financial straits. After being freed from prison through the intercession of the Earl of Oxford, Defoe found it necessary to write material of a more remunerative nature in order to pay his debts. And so his intermittent preoccupation with Selkirk's plight—the intriguing questions which he had thought about so often (How could he survive? How could he keep his sanity? How would he occupy his time?) developed into the full-length book in which he became so absorbed that fact and fiction became irrevocably entangled.

Though in modern times, Robinson Crusoe is thought of as being essentially a children's story, it was laden with religious and moral passages in its original version. The dialogue with Friday and the natives was the vehicle which Defoe used to convey the virtues of the spiritual life according to his Puritan convictions.

This first edition met with immediate popularity, and it has retained its appeal for more than two and a half centuries. It captured the imagination and fancy of young and old alike and started a rash of imitations which were soon labelled Robinsonades.

The Swiss Family Robinson. Perhaps the most famous Robinsonade is *The Swiss Family Robinson.* There are many differences as well as many similarities between the original story by Defoe and that created by the gentle and kindly Reverend Johann David Wyss, a Swiss clergyman. The Swiss saga is that of a group of people as opposed to the solitary Crusoe. Defoe wrote originally for adults, while the Reverend Wyss told a story to his children as an evening story, a tale that had been told to him by the captain of a small Russian sailing vessel. A fine raconteur, he enlarged and expanded the initial account and eventually wrote it all down. His son, Johann Rudolf, found the manuscript years later, and readied it for publication in 1812. Through many translations and additions by the translators, it eventually evolved as a work of several writers—a collaboration.

"Young Crusoes," "Rival Crusoes," "Boy Crusoes," and "Canadian Crusoes," among others, followed, but Defoe's *Robinson Crusoe* had the simplicity and narrative strength which has best withstood the test of time.

Alice's Adventures in Wonderland. This landmark in children's books has already been cited in this book. Suffice it to say that here we meet the famous literary Jekyl and Hyde, Charles Dodgson, a sober and dignified professor of mathematics who, at certain periods when he was creating, became Lewis Carroll, the playful prankster who concocted deliciously comical characters capable of wildly eccentric and amusing behavior. What is most significant, he created this enchantment when fun and fancy were rare commodities in books for children, thus starting a most beneficent trend.

The Merry Adventures of Robin Hood (1883). Merry, indeed, is that tale of those lovable rascals who took it upon themselves to aid the depressed peasants by thwarting the corruption of the noblemen and churchmen. Howard Pyle, the artist and the author, became absorbed in the pageantry and drama of medieval life. He studied the old legends and ballads and was able to recreate the sights, sounds, and characters of medieval England so realistically that the reader finds himself almost literally transported to Sherwood Forest with Robin Hood, Little John, Friar Tuck, and Maid Marian. Pyle's pen-and-ink drawings are masterly interpretations of his text.

History, drama, adventure! Howard Pyle brought all of this to children in a memorable literary work.

Treasure Island (1883). The year 1883 was a bonanza year for children's literature. The story of adventure and pirates that Lloyd Osborn asked his stepfather, Robert Louis Stevenson, to tell, "and no women, please, because they spoil a good story,"[23] was first issued as a serial in *Young Folks.* In 1883, it was brought out in book form under the title, *Treasure Island.*

While living at a health resort in Switzerland, and although homesick for his native Scotland and plagued by the ill health from which he had suffered all his life, Stevenson wove the romantic and exciting tale which was to become a milestone in juvenile literature because of the excellent craftsmanship which went into the telling.

With careful choice of words and phrases and rapid, continuous, exciting action, he created an adventure which involved unforgettable characters such as Billy Bones and Long John Silver.

In the Polynesian Islands where Stevenson lived for a time, he was affectionately called "Tusitala," teller of tales. His stories and poems have been a truly remarkable gift, not only to children of his day, but to generations of children since.

The Tale of Peter Rabbit. It is difficult to imagine that Beatrix Potter's *Tale of Peter Rabbit* met with the same initial negative reaction on the part of publishers as did Kenneth Grahame's *Wind in the Willows.* Story ideas using characters who were "ourselves in fur" were apparently not popular in those days. Consequently, Beatrix Potter had every child's friend, *Peter Rabbit,* privately printed as a small book with a picture in black and white on each page. Frederick Warne and Company requested permission to publish it when they noted the success of the first private printing. Beatrix Potter made colored drawings for this edition.

And so it was that a letter written to the oldest child of her former governess to entertain him when he was ill became the domain of all children "both in sickness and in health." The child is poor in experience, indeed, if he can't remember when he, at some time during his childhood, composed himself comfortably and waited expectantly for that familiar cue line which launches the story, "Once upon a time, there were four little rabbits, and their names were Flopsy, Mopsy, Cottontail, and Peter."

[23]Elizabeth Rider Montgomery, *The Story behind Great Books* (New York: Dodd, Mead & Co., 1946), p. 126.

The Tale of Peter Rabbit, published in 1902, *The Tale of Squirrel Nutkin,* and *The Tailor of Gloucester,* both published in 1903, are "classics in minature" created by Beatrix Potter, who had a certain empathy with children, understanding their thoughts and ways. She knew that they enjoyed having some things related to their size, *little* things that would fit into *their* world. And so she gave children "little" books with "big" stories in them.

❋   ❋   ❋

Elizabeth Nesbitt, commenting about the task of writing for children, noted that "those authors who have made their way into the hearts and minds of generations of children are often those who have not so much written a book as created a world peopled with unforgettable characters and filled with incidents which are right and inevitable."[24]

This statement seems to describe the books mentioned above, books which have survived the discriminating judgment of young readers as well as readers of all ages. Many more should be included: *Dr. Doolittle,* by Hugh Lofting, Kipling's *Jungle Tales* and *Just So Stories,* Mark Twain's *Tom Sawyer* and *Huckleberry Finn,* Louisa May Alcott's *Little Women,* Kenneth Grahame's *Wind in the Willows,* A. A. Milne's, *Winnie the Pooh,* and Wanda Gág's *Millions of Cats,* to mention but a few.

The list swells with the years. What a lovely literary road children may now travel as they become acquainted with the "survival of the fittest" in their literature and as they choose from the wealth of books which has been increasing with astonishing rapidity during the last hundred years.

This phenomenon is evident in children's libraries everywhere. Here is another youth room. This one is in Hawaii. Murals depicting the legends of ancient Hawaii cover the walls. They are the work of Juliette May Fraser, who painted them on wet plaster. We see Kana, stretching himself as thin as a cobweb and as tall as the sky, to bring back the sun, the moon, and the stars which had been hidden away by Kahoaalii to punish his people for their complaining.

And here is Kaukuikii, the poor little Menehune. He could not carry out his boast to catch the legs of the moon to make the night longer so that more work might be done. He was turned to stone as punishment for his bragging, and there he is, even to this day, on a mountain peak in Kauai.

These and other ancient Hawaiian gods and heroes are depicted larger than life-size in the lovely murals. The stories are between the covers of Padraic Colum's *The Bright Islands* and *At the Gateways of the Day.* On the shelves with these books of Hawaiian lore are myths, legends, and tales from other lands—China, Tibet, India, New Guinea, Spain, and countries the world over.

---

[24]Meigs, *Critical History of Children's Literature,* p. 345.

There are poetry collections and anthologies, too. Fiction for children of all ages abounds, books dealing with people and events of long ago and far away, as well as with people and events on the contemporary scene. One or two books on each shelf are set apart and opened to entice the casual or undecided browser. *The Secret Cargo* by Howard Pease, a hardy perennial in adventure, catches the eye as does the more recent book, a translation of *The Anchor of Mercy* by Pierre Macorlan. *The Weathermakers* by Ben Bova looks intriguing as does Robb White's *Surrender,* the story of action in the Philippine Islands during World War II.

There are shelves and shelves of non-fiction for juniors, too, with titles such as *Kings, Rulers and Statesmen, Captains of Industry,* and *The Story of Football,* and there are many, many books about basketball, badminton, volleyball, and baseball.

One sees *Pippi Longstocking, The Gammage Cup, Carry on Mr. Bowditch, The Perilous Road, Many Moons, This Boy Cody,* and others selected from the shelves to be the day's eye catchers.

Gulliver's Travels, Men of Iron, Shen of the Sea, the 1925 Newbery Award winner, and *The Castle of Llyr* are grouped on a shelf below a poster which invites children to COOL IT WITH BOOKS THIS SUMMER, JOIN THE NA LOU 'OLU 'OLU CLUB (pleasantly cool leaves). Some colorful paper leaves are attached to a thick branch in the middle of the room. On one side of each leaf is the title of a book. The other side identifies the grade and school which made the choice. If one were to judge from the number of leaves, it would appear that classes from all over the city had sent in their choices of "pleasantly cool leaves."

Low benches at low tilted racks make comfortable browsing for the littlest visitors as they turn the pages of *The Story of Babar, Where the Wild Things Are, Finders Keepers,* and other favorite picture storybooks.

A can of pencils, a box of cards, and a sign giving precise and simple directions for borrowing books are on each of two tables near the door.

The friendly surrounding is somehow familiar. It seems as though a whispered abracadabra or the soft caressing of an enchanted lamp might have magically transported the observer back to the youth room in the middle western library described in the opening pages of this book.

In these rooms and in all the other fine children's libraries throughout the country, young people find "times of wondering" and delight. They search, seek, explore, and discover. They also giggle and chuckle. They know they are wiser than Duvoisin's Petunia who only carries a book around the barnyard without reading it. They know, too, that read-

ing doesn't really "rot the mind" as Tim McGrath in Robert Lawson's
Rabbit Hill stated. They realize that Robert Lawson is deliberately tick-
ling their funny bones, and they suspect that Tim McGrath might really
like to read.

Today's children and youth have this opportunity to explore the
treasury of books which is their heritage because Caxton, Boreman,
Newbery, and Harris thought about publishing to please "the little
masters and mistresses" of years gone by; because Bewick and his successors gave of their talents to illustrate books for them; and because
Lewis Carroll, Rudyard Kipling, A. A. Milne, and a host of others who
followed them respected children's individuality and their need to have
a literature of their own.

QUESTIONS AND SUGGESTIONS

1. Select two or three publishing houses which publish children's trade
   books.
   a. Procure lists of their publications.
   b. Choose a few titles from each publisher and thoughtfully appraise
      their content, style, and illustrations.
   c. What similarities do you discover? Are there any identifiable
      differences which suggest publisher's preferences?
2. Select several distinguished contemporary children's book artists.
   Compare their work with that of some of the earlier artists cited in
   this chapter. Are there any common criteria which might be applied
   to both groups?
3. What books do you remember reading and rereading when you
   were a child? Try to remember what made these books especially
   appealing to you. Which of the contemporary children's books have
   special appeal for you? Compare these with your early favorites. Do
   they have any common characteristics?
4. Read three or four of the "books which have lived." Which of the
   books published since 1940 can you identify as those most likely to
   endure the test of time? What seem to be the basic qualities inherent
   in memorable and enduring books?

SELECTED REFERENCES FOR CHILDREN

ALEXANDER, LLOYD. *The Castle of Llyr.* New York: Holt, Rinehart & Winston,
     1966.
BOVA, BEN. *The Weathermakers.* New York: Holt, Rinehart & Winston, 1967.
DE BRUNHOFF, JEAN. *The Story of Babar.* New York: Random House, 1937.
CHRISMAN, ARTHUR. *Shen of the Sea.* New York: E. P. Dutton, 1925.
COLUM, PADRAIC. *At the Gateways of the Day.* New Haven, Conn.: Yale
     University Press, 1924.
————. *The Bright Islands.* New Haven, Conn.: Yale University Press, 1925.
DUVOISIN, ROGER. *Petunia.* New York: Alfred A. Knopf, 1950.

KENDALL, CAROL. *The Gammage Cup.* New York: Harcourt, Brace & World, 1959.

LATHAM, JEAN LEE. *Carry on Mr. Bowditch.* Boston: Houghton Mifflin Co., 1955.

LAWSON, ROBERT. *Rabbit Hill.* New York: Viking Press, 1944.

LECKIE, ROBERT. *The Story of Football.* New York: Random House, 1965.

LINDGREN, ASTRID. *Pippi Longstocking.* New York: Viking Press, 1950.

LIPKIND, WILLIAM, and MORDVINOFF, NICOLAS. (pseud., WILL and NICOLAS). *Finders Keepers.* New York: Harcourt, Brace & World, 1960.

MACORLAN, PIERRE. *The Anchor of Mercy.* New York: Pantheon Books, 1967.

PEASE, HOWARD. *The Secret Cargo.* Garden City, N.Y.: Doubleday & Co., 1946.

PYLE, HOWARD. *Men of Iron.* New York: Harper & Row, 1891.

SENDAK, MAURICE. *Where the Wild Things Are.* New York: Harper & Row, 1963.

STEELE, WILLIAM O. *The Perilous Road.* New York: Harcourt, Brace & World, 1958.

SWIFT, JONATHAN. *Gulliver's Travels.* Many editions from which to choose.

THURBER, JAMES. *Many Moons.* New York: Harcourt, Brace & World, 1943.

WEISBERGER, BERNARD, and NEVINS, A. *Captains of Industry.* New York: American Heritage Junior Library, Harper & Row, 1966.

WHITE, ROBB. *Surrender.* Garden City, N.Y.: Doubleday & Co., 1966.

WILSON, LEON. *This Boy Cody.* New York: Franklin Watts, 1950.

WISE, L. F., and EGAN, E. W., eds. *Kings, Rulers and Statesmen.* New York: Sterling Publishing Co., 1967.

SELECTED CHAPTER REFERENCES

HEAL, SIR AMBROSE. *The English Writing Masters and Their Copy Books.* Cambridge, England: Cambridge University Press, n.d.

MAHONY, BERTHA E.; LATIMER, LOUISE P.; and FOLMSBEE, BEULAH. *Illustrators of Children's Books, 1744-1945.* Boston: Horn Book, 1947.

MEIGS, CORNELIA; EATON, ANNE; NESBITT, ELIZABETH; and VIGUERS, RUTH HILL. *A Critical History of Children's Literature.* New York: Macmillan Co., 1953.

MONTGOMERY, ELIZABETH RIDER. *The Story behind Great Books.* New York: Dodd, Mead & Co., 1946.

MUIR, PERCY. *English Children's Books: 1600-1900.* New York: Frederick A. Praeger, Publishers, 1954.

NEWBERY, JOHN. *A Little Pretty Pocket-Book.* New York: Harcourt, Brace & World, 1967.

OPIE, IONA and PETER. *The Oxford Book of Nursery Rhymes.* Oxford: The Clarendon Press, 1951.

SLOANE, WILLIAM. *Children's Books in England and America in the Seventeenth Century.* New York: King's Crown Press, Columbia University Press, 1955.

STONE, WILLIAM. *The Gigantick Histories of Thomas Boreman.* Portland, Maine: Southworth Press, 1933.

THWAITE, M. F. "John Newbery and his first book for children," introductory essay to Newbery, John. *A Little Pretty Pocket-Book.* New York: Harcourt, Brace & World, 1967.

Photographs courtesy of Gladys
Eisele.

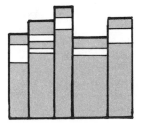

index